Foreword by
PHIL SIMM

Superbowl MVP, NFL Sports Analyst, Former New York Giant

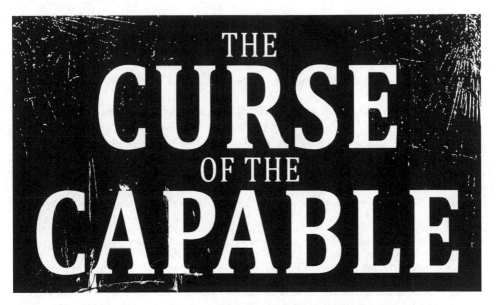

THE
CURSE
OF THE
CAPABLE

The Hidden Challenge to a Balanced, Healthy, High-Achieving Life

DR. ARTHUR P. CIARAMICOLI

WITH JOHN ALLEN MOLLENHAUER

NEW YORK

THE **CURSE** OF THE **CAPABLE**
The Hidden Challenge to a Balanced, Healthy, High-Achieving Life

by DR. ARTHUR P. CIARAMICOLI
© 2010 Dr. Arthur P. Ciara,icoli. All rights reserved.

Library of Congress Cataloging in-Publication Data:
Ciaramicoli, Arthur
The Curse of the Capable: The Hidden Challenges to a Balanced, Healthy, High-Achieving Life
p. cm.
ISBN 978-1-60037-662-7 (Paperback)
ISBN 978-1-60037-663-4 (Hardcover)
1. Self Help 2. Psychology 3. Body, Mind, Spirit
2009936590

Printed and bound in the United States of America

Published by:
MBO® Productions
An Imprint of Morgan James Publishing
1225 Franklin Ave. Ste 325
Garden City, NY 11530-1693
Toll Free 800-485-4943
www.MorganJamesPublishing.com

Cover Design by David Grau

Interior Design by Deborah Carraro

What people are saying about
The Curse of the Capable

"I don't cry easily but I couldn't hold back the tears as I read about all the people who have struggled with the Curse and never known the way out. After seeing several psychiatrists', trying different meds and never feeling better I had lost hope. Then somehow I joined the group and the understanding and relief began slowly and has never stopped. The book reminds me of how compulsive achievement was for me, and how breaking free has given me the satisfaction in my life that has always been missing. You always say empathy is the key to success, it took my legal mind several months to believe you and I think you have given the reader many examples to make a most convincing case that without knowing how to enter the world of others we are lost in space."

- Rebecca S.
Attorney

"Success at all costs is really not success at all and often leaves communities, families and lives in its vast depleted wake. If you have lived as a depleted high achiever, you probably know this already. But the BIG question is… what do you do about it? The Curse is a trap with no easy way out…until now! Dr. Ciaramicoli and Coach Mollenhauer have put together a deeply provocative game plan for true success like nothing I have seen before. In each stage you'll discover insight, touching examples and juicy questions that reveal the core dynamics of "the curse". Understand them so you can PLAY the games of your life again with joy, resiliency and full self-expression, and win."

- Coach Dave Buck
CEO CoachVille.com

"My only regret in reading *The Curse of the Capable* Dr. C is that you didn't write it ten years ago. Today I am mostly free of the obsessive drive to succeed at all costs but if I had known years ago what stages I needed to understand to make myself comfortable in my own skin I could have saved my marriage and been a better father. I hope every driven person who is misdirected to obtain love reads your book, the journal questions are challenging and they make you very thoughtful about what motivates your behavior. What a great compliment to our group experience. The stories are very moving and of course I recognized some of the people including myself. As I read through I felt hopeful for myself and all those like me who are capable but could never find the real key to success"

- Frank M.
Owner of Construction Company

"Being a high-achiever doesn't mean squat if you're not healthy. Moreover, the healthier you are, the more you achieve. This book is a wakeup call and the antidote for those of us that are consumed by the fast pace of today's world. But it won't slow you down. In fact, it'll put you on a fast train to the ultimate in well-being---complete health and substantial wealth."

- Michael Port
New York Times Bestselling Author of
"The Think Big Manifesto"

"As I read through the book, I also realized again how thankful I am and how blessed I am to be one of your patients. The stories are so powerful and of course as a group member I have personally witnessed the transformation of people, like myself, from being cursed to being free to live to our true potential. I wish that all those who have been trying so hard all their lives and yet never feeling complete would read and study the four stages outlined in your new book. I think if everyone would read my favorite chapter "The Spiritual Learner" we could bring about harmony in our world. Thank you for your patience and wisdom and for understanding what no one seemed to grasp in all my efforts to feel more fulfilled."

- Linda M.
Project Manager

"Understanding who you are becomes paramount to taking care of yourself. Making lifestyle choices *begin* with self-awareness, the story you tell about your life and how you are in the world. If this story is not supportive, it gives rise to Performance Addiction and a spectrum of unhealthy lifestyle choices which lead to the problems we see every day. This book, *The Curse of the Capable* enables people to gain insight into this not well explored or explained cycle of personal destruction that can occur even amongst the most accomplished. It is a great book to read if you want to live a balanced and healthy lifestyle, successfully."

- Dr. Suzanne Steinbaum D.O
SRSHEART.COM Director, Women and
Heart Disease Heart and Vascular Institute
Lenox Hill Hospital, New York

"This important book shows how the quest for impressive achievements can lead many down the path to unhappiness and self-destruction. This book is a must read for those wanting a better understanding of the human potential for self-peace and happiness that is obtainable by all. After all, our physical health is dependent on many factors, including our intimate and caring relationship with others and our mastery over our competitive drives that could sabotage those relationships."

- Joel Fuhrman, MD.
Author, *Eat to Live* and *Eat for Health*,
Family Physician, & Nutritional
Researcher.

"As I read *The Curse of the Capable* I thought of the people I've known and others I haven't known that haven't been as fortunate as I and others in group. I thought of the star athlete you and I know who took her own life after a sports loss and how it might have been for her had someone like you been in her life. As I read through each of the 4 stages my heart swelled after each story and burst after each success which I know personally. I wanted to say this - You are a blessing Dr. C. A blessing for Anthony and me, Gina and the countless other lives you've touched. Nothing in life could ever compare to the significance of what you've done and continue to do for others – not a pro baseball contract, not running 50 marathons, not even a doctorate degree or writing a book or anything else for that matter could EVER compare. This book is your best ever!"

- John H.
Northeast Sales Manager

"I drove my business to the top, working 80 hour weeks, traveling frequently and when I finally arrived I told my partner I felt Cursed. Why? No inner peace and just more to do every day, not at all like I imagined. I neglected my wife and children, all the while thinking we would all be happy once I was successful, had loads of money and a bigger house. Well, Dr. C, your book and your work has proven I, like many others, have been living according to a myth that drives each of us into the ground. I am proud to be one of the stories in your new book, proud because I am an example of someone who was lost and now who has learned the skills to be on the road to peace of mind. Your book, like your groups, requires hard work, nothing achievers will balk at but it is a different kind of work. It is work for the soul and the heart. Something I knew little about. Everyone will benefit from this book that makes the commitment to open up and learn. Congratulations!"

- Tom K.
Retired CEO

"What a good book! At first I wondered why I should care about all the dysfunctional stories illustrated from Dr. C's client experiences. Then I saw the *pattern* of the Curse that all of us today experience. Taking off my own *mask*, I found words that explain the *journey* and pearls of *wisdom* that will help me improve my own healthy, high achieving life. There are great insights in this book that are worthy for *reflection*. Read it; you will be *encouraged and freed*."

- Paul J. Hindelang
President, Results-Systems Corporation

"*The Curse of the Capable* unveils the mystery of why capable people sometimes choose to live beyond the edge of their own health and well-being. In the stories of the *Capable* and through the accompanying reflective and active exercises in this book, we are empowered to glimpse our own fervent desire for a more vital life, to sharpen our budding insights, and to write a new chapter in the story of our personal and professional strivings. I can think of no better way to wake-up-into the life you've already worked so hard to build than to read and act on the wisdom you'll find in this book."

- Catherine Pastille MA, MBA, Ph.D.
Business Administration President,
The Hope Research Center, Inc.
Smithfield, RI

"Happiness, the light that we all seek, may be elusive at times but the mere knowledge that there is such a mental state gives us hope to be and to do better. This book gives us a path to that end. Read it, to see for yourself."

- T. Colin Campbell Ph.D
Jacob Gould Schurman Professor Emeritus
of Nutritional Biochemistry, Cornell
University Ithaca, NY, Author
"*The China Study*"

"The insights in Dr. Ciaramicoli's book Performance Addiction were profound in terms of corporate success. Now, with his new book, he has captured the essence of what drives us toward success at all costs. Many in the corporate world feel cursed and I, as a senior manager, have benefited greatly by reading and understanding the lives of Dr. Ciaramicoli's clients as they work toward more complete health. Each story seems to convey a new way of succeeding in a stressful environment, especially as he describes the challenges we must all negotiate for solid self worth. I have recommended "The Curse of the Capable" to all my employees and will continue to learn from re-reading its content. This book goes far beyond the typical self help book to provide real ways of feeling balanced while operating on a very high level"

- Richard Werner
Senior Director, Data Center Management,
Comcast Headquarters, Philadelphia.

"I have been following Dr. Ciaramicoli's work since his publication of The Power of Empathy in 2000. His ability to understand the heart and soul of high achievers is quite amazing. The stories of his clients in his new book are poignant, heartfelt and full of the wisdom and insight that will lead good, talented people with the Curse to a level of happiness that has eluded them all of their lives. Dr. Ciaramicoli's shares the strategies that will bring achievers the life they have always longed for while unleashing their highest potential in the process."

- Robert Cherney, Ph.D.
LADC1, Chief Psychologist, Advocates
Community Counseling Services,
Framingham, Massachusetts.

"Are you feeling stressed, drained, and low on energy and satisfaction? The *addiction* to *performance* may be robbing you of the life you deserve. If a substance were turning your life upside down, at some point you'd be forced to make real changes. But when your "substance" is peak-performance the odds are not nearly so good. *The Curse of the Capable* has cracked the code to understanding why it can be so hard to change your lifestyle; it's like a drink of water after years of running full speed in the desert. It lifts the burden and sets you on the path to creating *a lifestyle that supports your performance* rather than continuing the performance at the cost of your life."

- Shawn Phillips
CEO FullStrengthLIFE.com;
Author, *Strength for Life*

"Providing a roadmap to change from the inside out, *The Curse of the Capable* is worth its weight in gold to achievers. Applying psychological theory to real life, this book is a mini course on how and why our (inner) psychology drives our (outer) behavior. Dr. Ciaramicoli demonstrates the ability of people to get beyond their hidden struggles with heartbreaking clinical cases. This is not a book; rather this is a manual for personal change. Each chapter has provocative questions and specific actions to take toward revising your inner novel. Use this manual to rewrite your story, break the curse, and enjoy life!"

- Jeffrey A. Betman, Ph.D.
Licensed Psychologist

"At a time in our nation when so much importance is placed on doing and creating more, The Curse of the Capable shifts one's attention to "balance and beingness" and dares to challenge long standing societal beliefs about fulfillment and happiness. The message that touches my core in this book is very clear, "any positive change I seek in my world must happen within me first". The Curse of the Capable will inspire many!"

- Vince Falone, LMT, CST,
Co-founder of Center for Relaxation and
Healing, and Co-leader candidate in, the
Mankind Project International MKP.org

"Take heart...what a difference this book can make in your life! "The Curse" is true...we are a society so focused on professional excellence that we have forgotten what true excellence really means. The answers of how we can be living for unconditional happiness and a fulfilling life await you in this wonderful book. Dr Ciaramicoli has created a must read for every parent, young adult and anyone who is "successful" but still feeling a bit empty inside."

- Rob Poulos
Founder Zero to Hero Fitness and Author of
the Fat Burning Furnace.

"A rich insight in *The Curse of the Capable* is that 'Only through the honest feedback of others can we discover the truth of who we really are.'. Dr. Ciaramicoli and John Allen Mollenhauer weave a practical path for taking that insight to action. Journaling the questions they pose with an honest and open heart can lead powerfully to that discovery experience, and I thank them for this book!"

- Thomas Houle
Senior Director Consumer Insight
& Strategy Kraft Foods (ret.),
Center Director of The Mankind Project
International, New Jersey

"This is a must read book if you ever want to live a lifestyle that works for you. The Curse of the Capable hits on the key aspects of lifestyle that most people don't see. They are hidden and they are driving you, maybe non-stop. Why wait until you've accomplished a goal before you start living the lifestyle you want and need, to look and feel better, and function at healthy levels? In my business I have clients tell me as soon as they are done with a project or the summer is over they will start to exercise. They are missing the boat! Dr. Ciaramicoli and John Allen Mollenhauer have written a literal road map to getting free of what prevents people from being able to perform well, with real quality of life

- Eddie Enriquez
Founder CAP Elite, Co-Founder
MyTrainer.com and PerformanceLifestyle
Professional.

"Wow! *The Curse of the Capable* explains, in exact detail, the biggest challenges faced with high achievers and how to break through stopping points along the way. I was immediately taken in by the real-life examples of extremely talented people who had found themselves stuck in one point of their lives and how changing their perspective could immediately release them from their self-imposed bonds. A great read for anyone who wants more in their personal and professional life!"

- **Kevin Gianni**
Health Advocate and Author *"High Raw:*
A Simple Approach to Health, Eating
and Saving the Planet"

"In this ground-breaking book, readers discover the true power of interpersonal communication to heal, move forward, and have a fulfilling and happy life at work and at home. Perception and empathy along with a true understanding of the factors causing even those who are highly successful to feel inadequate, anxious, and dissatisfied with life are what will allow readers the chance to finally re-write their personal narratives and communicate from a new place of inner wisdom!"

- **Felicia J. Slattery, M.A., M.Ad.Ed**
Communication Consultant, Founder
www.CommunicationTransformation.com

"Wouldn't it be great to be able to repair your own car, fix the lawn mower, write a book, start a web page, manage our own finances, and be in total control? As a nation we spend billions of dollars on how-to books all for the sake of becoming more capable; by why? What's driving you to do it all yourself? Dr Ciaramicoli and John Allen Mollenhauer brilliantly capture the often over-looked and underestimated reasons why so many of us want to become so capable thinking we have to "do it all."

- **Tom Terwilliger**
Experience the Leap Executive Coach,
Former Mr. America, and once
overworked do-it-yourselfer
ExperienceTheLeap.com

DEDICATION

To My Mother, My Unsung Hero
Carmella (Camie) Marie

ACKNOWLEDGEMENTS

Every significant accomplishment in my life would not have been attained without the love, support and guidance of others. My wife Karen of 29 years has always been the person who has given me objective feedback from a position of love and compassion.

Throughout our lives your honesty has been my saving grace. I thank you once again for being a constant support and believer in my work and in me as a person. Your editorial comments have been most helpful. You have encouraged me to write *The Curse of the Capable* for several years and now with your consistent support it is a reality. One of the key purposes of this book is to come to a truthful understanding of oneself through the eyes of others who have the ability to be objective. You have given me this gift, with love, repeatedly.

Our daughter Alaina read and edited every line of the manuscript with keen insight. Your insightful eye as an educator alerted me to the profound effect of perfectionism on young hearts and spirits. Your constant support, always asking, "Dad how's the writing going", means more than you can imagine. I also benefited significantly from your master's thesis pointing out the difficulties of children growing up in our fast paced culture. Your young students are extremely fortunate to have a teacher with such an open heart and excellent insight into the kind of environment that creates sound emotional development.

I also want to thank our daughter Erica for her support and love. Your ability to care for the mentally challenged with patience and sensitivity fuels my belief that anyone can make changes if given the right opportunity. Your clients are fortunate to have your caring smile in their lives on a daily basis. Very few counselors have the dedication and compassion to work with the chronically ill and you are one of the gifted who remains optimistic for their future regardless of the bleak histories you read in their medical charts.

My partner and good friend John Allen Mollenhauer has participated in the formation and construction of this book from the beginning. Many long conversations helped establish the proper sequence of the book, and with John's encouragement we decided to make reference to my previous works as a foundation for understanding "*the curse*" in all its complexities. John Allen's expertise in energy management provided an important accent to the symptoms of *the curse* and his own personal experience (highlighted on our web site) of recovery during the writing of this book provided me with constructive feedback to each section. His comments were based on his actual experiences of the writing as the book progressed, allowing for insight of a very real nature as John progressed through each phase of the work himself. His expertise in PerformanceLifestyle training and coaching was easily integrated into the major premises of *the curse*.

Karen O'Donnell Taylor, educator and writer, made the most significant editorial contribution to the text, completely changing the tone of the book to a more readable, concise manuscript.

My friends Linda Hood and Lori Roback both provided unique insights and editorial comments that were integrated into the text. Both Linda and Lori displayed unusual understanding of the theoretical aspects of the book

Our Publisher, Deborah Micek, at MBO® Productions, was an energetic believer from the beginning and her excellent command of the world of new media marketing has been most beneficial. Her administrator and Web designer, Deborah Carraro has also been most helpful. In addition she helped me continue to expand my Italian language skills

David Hancock, CEO of Morgan James, also provided significant enthusiasm for this project from the start. I am particularly appreciative of working with a publisher who truly understands the content of the work. Director of Operations Jim Howard, Author Relations consultant. Margo Toulouse, designer David Austin Grau and the entire Morgan James staff have been very helpful throughout the entire publication process.

I am very thankful to my long time circle of family and friends who have supported me through this writing process: Janice and Jimmy Blackler, Doreen and Bryan Constantino, Jeanne and Mark Fitzpatrick, Gerri and Richard Tessicini, Dianne and Richard Werner, and Donna, Lisa and Philip Wood.

My good friend and exercise buddy Mike Chagnon has consistently supported my writing and encouraged me in the process.

My friend and fellow author, Dr. Pier Massimo Forni contributed supportive and practical advice in regards to the applicability of the book to the general audience.

Dr. Jim Brennan, kindly read through the manuscript and immediately knew my favorite chapter was "the Spiritual Learner". Your encouragement to elaborate on the heart of this book in the future has been most meaningful to me.

Dr. Catherine Pastille also spent significant time reviewing the manuscript and clearly understood the need for this book from her extensive experience in the corporate and academic world.

My good friend Larry Brady, a former Academic All-American and professional athlete, helped deepen my perspective regarding the energy and concentration needed to perform on such high levels with consistency.

A special thanks to Phil Simms for taking time out of his busy schedule to read the manuscript and write the foreword. If anyone knows about the in's and out's of high achievement, it is you. You relate from a position of humility which, in my experience, is unusual for those who have attained such stature, a lesson to us all. It has been a privilege and an honor to have met you.

My colleagues Dr. Robert Cherney, Dr Valerie Sawyer-Smith, and Dr. Peter Smith have always been most supportive of my work.

Lastly I am most appreciative to the wonderful people who come to me and allow me to help in their quest towards balanced living. It is always a reciprocal process; at times I wonder who gains more. Thank you all!

FOREWORD

Most of my life I have been around people who achieve at high levels. I am not talking exclusively about professional athletes or media professionals. I am also talking about the local gym teacher or school nurse, the local farmer, the mom who fed all of us after a day of practice, managed to work part time and be a wonderful wife and friend without ever complaining. They all seemed to perform with great success as far as I could see.

I always wondered, particularly after spending 15 years in the National Football League, how some very capable people had such difficulty managing their health, relationships, parenting and marriages when they were outside of their comfort zone, when they were not achieving in the areas where they knew they excelled. Over the years I noticed that those who could perform at high levels and lead balanced lives were clearly in the minority.

I have seen many talented people in all walks of life compromise their emotional health by eating, drinking or behaving in some other excessive manner, ultimately leading to feelings of unhappiness.

I have seen the faces of high achievers look depleted and worn out despite continuing to perform without anyone knowing how overwhelmed they feel.

I started reading *The Curse of the Capable* on a plane ride home from the west coast. After the first few chapters, I had to get up out of my seat and walk a bit to settle my mind. I couldn't believe that someone had finally identified what I had wondered about for years.

Dr. Ciaramicoli has obviously immersed himself in the lives of achievers for a very long time. He has revealed the hidden challenges we all must face, and particularly has identified the strategies for those who feel *Cursed* to finally succeed in leading the kind of life they have probably desired most of their adult years.

Achievers finally have a map to guide them to overall success, not just success in their chosen fields. The road to achieve with balance and health has never before been outlined with the clear, easy-to-apply strategies contained in this book.

"*The curse*" not only gives all of us a way of understanding how the past holds us down but the lessons derived from this book can help each of us understand where we are stuck and how to work things out so our spirits can remain high.

I won't divulge to you which chapter epitomizes my persona. You'll have to keep reading to figure it out. But I will encourage you to honestly answer the questions at each chapter's conclusion and pass it on to anyone whose health and happiness you deeply care about. I think it will make you a better person, husband, wife, parent, coach and friend.

Phil Simms
Super Bowl MVP,
NFL Sports Analyst
Former New York Giant

CONTENTS

3RD STAGE–ACKNOWLEDGE THE EMOTIONAL IMPACT OF YOUR STORY: THE 6 TRIALS OF ADULTHOOD.

4TH STAGE–RECOGNIZE HOW YOUR STORY DISTORTS YOUR THINKING

PREFACE

Discover what achievers all over the world are realizing:

The story you created about yourself early in life, which is part fiction, is having a dramatic impact on your present lifestyle—how you think and live.

The assumption that all capable people in our culture have peace of mind and are satisfied with their life course is commonplace. Is this notion true? Not always. In fact millions have fallen prey to a belief system that says appearance and status provide the golden road to love and respect. Driven by their version of this story in an attempt to perfect themselves, they are hiding their self doubt through constant achievement at the cost of losing balance and wellbeing.

Suffering from being overwhelmed emotionally and physically, exhausted and fatigued, often with the health complications of being overweight; they have felt deeply disappointed.

The Curse of the Capable describes how a biased view of your self can lead to a fragile sense of self, addictive thinking and behavior, and a seemingly mysterious downward spiral that the majority of people can't see or untangle.

Dr. Arthur P. Ciaramicoli, author of the books The Power of Empathy and Performance Addiction, has spent the last 30 years studying, treating, and freeing capable people from all walks of life from the personal, story-driven challenges that ruin the lives of otherwise intelligent talented people.

What leads to a personal story that creates a confused condition and ultimately hinders successful living?

In The Curse of the Capable you will read about men and women who long for intimacy and strive for perfection in an effort to please those around them. Ultimately they feel defeated, depleted of energy, and misunderstood; all while feeling obligated to perform for others at all costs.

This book helps you understand and appreciate the internal stories that are running your life. It reveals the resulting, yet hidden challenges that are preventing you, a capable person, from taking better care of yourself and other aspects of your life.

Each challenge is discussed through the poignant stories of everyday achievers from diverse backgrounds: housewives, lawyers, teachers, contractors, models, trainers, doctors, media personnel, corporate executives, as well as professional athletes.

Ultimately, this book reveals the four stages to changing your story for greater love, health and success.

Lifestyle Trainer and coach, John Allen Mollenhauer, founder of PerformanceLifestyle.com, after discovering Dr Ciaramicoli's original work Performance Addiction, discovered that he too was living with "the curse".

While on the mend, his quest and contribution to this book helped define the curse and how it manifests as a physical condition, shedding further light on why getting free is essential to living a fully engaged life with peace of mind.

This book will guide you in creating a balanced, healthy, high-achieving life, free of the guilt and tension of the past that is driving you a little crazy.

Introduction:
What Is Wrong
With Me?

Yesterday, as I was driving to an appointment, one of my clients called crying and in crisis. Linda is a 50 year old elementary teacher and single mom. Her son had just informed her that he'd been arrested for cocaine possession the night before and needed her help. He had previously impregnated two girl friends and 28 year-old Bobby could barely make his child support payments.

Linda had been feeling overwhelmed before this call. She was very discouraged by her weight gain over the last few years and was hating menopause. She was feeling like she would never meet a "good man," encountering men on match that "can't put two grammatically correct sentences together." She felt she could not hold up much longer.

Her second job of managing an accountant's books was taking all her time on weeknights and weekends. Linda is the "go to" person in her large family. She is the one who took care of her dying father for several months, feeding and bathing him. She did this despite the fact he could never find anything right with any of his kids. Her last memory of her dad was telling him she loved him on his death bed as he angrily responded by saying "I love everyone in my family." She longed to hear him say "I love you," not "I love everyone," but it never happened. Her lifelong wish was just to hear him say "I love you Linda".

As a high school senior she became pregnant and he didn't speak to her for 4 years. As a young girl she would iron his shirts in their cold basement hoping that when he came home from work, he would be pleased. However, he never said a word. It was simply expected. His critical temper was always a threat in the house. As a result, she became driven to accomplish and achieve in the hopes of some day winning his approval. His typical, non-supportive reactions to her are embedded in her soul.

Linda could never quite please any man she became involved with. Her ex-husband left her when Bobby was four. He hid money in his construction business so whenever big bills were due for his sons, he claimed he had little money available.

I have known Linda for several months. She is the kind of person who would defend you in a battle. She is intelligent, creative, attractive but also quite driven, somewhat obsessed with her fading appearance, can't seem to relax, always on the go, and always doing a favor for someone. Yet she lives a life devoid of love and happiness. Her health is deteriorating.

Linda is a constant achiever but at an overwhelming cost. In this phone call, she asked me the question she has asked so many, many times. "I try so very hard! What is wrong with me?"

As I talked with Linda on this day, I realized that she was talking about a scenario I have heard many times, from people of all walks of life. She has *"The Curse* of the Capable." This capable woman has helped thousands of children love the process of learning. She has raised three children on her own, all becoming college graduates. She has earned the respect of colleagues and friends alike.

Though she has accomplished so much she still requires more and more achievement to prove herself worthy. This overachievement was contributing to the demise of her own well being, a pattern she has experienced throughout her life.

We, the capable ones, tend to become invested in curing others, solving problems and looking good, when in fact, we are really making efforts to vicariously heal ourselves.

You will hear many stories of my clients suffering from the *"Curse"* as I have spent the last 30 years studying, treating and freeing capable people from all walks of life from the challenges that ruin the lives of otherwise intelligent, talented people.

I have met and treated thousands of capable people who embody the qualities that are highly regarded in personal and professional life. Yet they do not seem to appreciate what they have or what they accomplish. Plagued by low self esteem they cannot solve an internal problem with external achievement, no matter how hard they try.

We Teach Our Own Struggle

I am intimately familiar with the curse of overachievement as a means to gain love and respect. Growing up I often doubted how my parents felt about me. I now know, as an adult, how very much they loved me and how they sacrificed everything they could for my welfare.

In the early part of my life, however, I had much doubt as to the constancy of their love. My mother, even though she was very loving, placed an inordinate weight on appearance, image and how we looked to the neighbors and relatives. My dad, on the other hand, placed great emphasis on athletic ability and had little tolerance for less than exceptional performance. He often told me I needed to "do something big in the world."

I didn't realize then that they thought they were helping me to become a better person. When I was younger, appearance and performance seemed to be the key to maintaining their love.

Over time I learned that my perceptions and fears were incorrect. On many occasions as I grew older, they demonstrated that their love was unwavering. As I matured it was easier to feel the love of my mother for my just "being there".

It took longer for me to experience that unconditional sense of love from my father. After my mother died, my father became more vulnerable and his soft side came forth.

My story about myself was distorted. I thought that love was based on how functional one person is to another. It left me with the idea that, as long as I was doing for others, and performing in ways that earned their approval, I would be cared for. It became very difficult for me to believe anyone would love me for who I am and not for what I do.

Today I can say I was loved for just being my parent's son. Until I edited my early story however, I could not accept the love of others as not being exclusively based on what functional value I may have had for them.

The hardwiring we adopt as young people can plague us for life unless we have the courage to re-examine who we are in adulthood. We need to re-edit the initial story we created. Only through the honest feedback of others can we discover the truth of who we really are.

As you read though this book, you will come to understand why I place great value on group feedback and of gaining a consensus of opinion about ourselves from objective, reasonable people. Limiting ourselves to the feedback of a few can be dangerous. I will tell you about several individuals who have gained freedom from "*the curse*" through honest, intense interactions with others. Linda has recently joined one of my group-coaching sessions. I believe her participation will lead to the freedom she has longed for her entire life.

This book was written for achievers for a reason. Achievers tend to be forward-moving, highly capable people who tend to mask hardships, not having the time, space, energy or tools to cope more effectively. They keep moving forward and their hidden problems get worse. The suffering that is covered up drives them to accomplish and achieve more. They end up trading health for success for the wrong reasons.

In my clinical practice, it is a lack of balance and well-being that has a domino effect on the energy, health and fitness of virtually every "capable" client. Despite having relative success, these achievers don't feel successful as their "curse" drives them to overspend their energy, and this brings negative consequences.

It is important to emphasize that, despite many of my clients being preoccupied with money and material gain (particularly my male clients,) this is not a syndrome that is reserved for the rich. I see a diverse group of people in my practice. Those suffering from *the curse* come from many walks of life. From CEO's to professional athletes to schoolteachers and housewives, the hidden challenges you are about to become aware of are at play. It is literally a Western phenomenon with very few people in our culture excluded from membership.

They know they should take better care of themselves. They know a great deal about what they *should be doing*. Yet, for some reason, they just don't seem to be able to achieve their goals in a balanced, healthy way. When they make the attempt to do so, these intelligent people buy into so-called solutions, such as obsessive diets or overly structured exercise regimens that do little more than reinforce the very problem they need to solve. They stay on this downward trend albeit with some gain in the short term., but because they are not dealing with the real problem and are just "doing" more, they end up running in circles.

It is the chicken or the egg situation. They need to live better, but can't. Lack of practical know-how aside, they are so driven they just can't stop. Why? Because saying simply think positive, get more sleep, eat better and exercise more is not solving the problem. It's not even touching upon their emotional distress or what's causing it. The challenges that are driving them are hidden. They are not obvious or easy to identify, let alone deal with once and for all if you don't know how to treat them. When you can't get to the source of your problem, in a manner of speaking, you feel *cursed*, don't you?

For capable, forward-moving people, this creates depression, especially when their achievements are never good enough. Paradoxically they're trying to fix a problem that achievement alone isn't designed to solve.

It's seemingly easier to deal with the symptoms of *"the curse."* The real challenge is to solve the underlying problem, which is worth every ounce of time and energy expended. If you incorporate the insights described in this book, gleaned from my own journey and the lives of many of my clients, I believe you will have the tools to solve the real problem plaguing your present situation, for which I have coined the phrase, *"The Curse of the Capable."*

Dropping the Weight of Your Past

The curse is often driven by the weight of the past, incessant ruminating around unresolved emotional issues that are not clearly understood. Many people seeking psychological help through therapy, reading, workshops etc lack a context to provide needed perspective and a game plan so-to-speak. Without this perspective they find themselves on a never-ending quest to solve a problem from their past that they don't understand. And nothing makes your life harder than trying to overcome something you are unclear about that is depleting your very essence and energy. Not knowing what it is or what to do about it will prompt you to try anything in desperation. Finally you may just give up trying to resolve the issues, rolling your eyes back at the mere suggestion.

I do not believe in belaboring the past as most people have experienced without resolve, but I do believe your emotions will tell you where the past is interfering with the present. Those places are where you want to spend your time and this book will likely prompt you to address those areas. My hope is that, after you answer the questions that follow each chapter and read how my clients have resolved this dilemma, you will emerge with new insight and direction toward a more liberated life.

In today's fast-paced day and age, doing the emotional work as I am detailing is part of improving your lifestyle. Your lifestyle is comprised of *how you think, feel* and *live*. For achievers in particular, cleaning up the past, which is affecting how you think and live today, is like getting your house in order; getting to the root of dysfunctional thinking and perceiving so you can feel better.

Whether your present situation is mild or extreme, it's about getting a few people in your corner. They can empathize, acknowledge your suffering and help you reinforce new, richer ways of being. It's about helping you rewrite your story with a new, more accurate view of yourself. This creates freedom. Covering up keeps you stuck. Though being vulnerable may be painful for you, doing this work will gain you freedom from *the curse*!

Almost all the hidden challenges that comprise *the curse* are universal, even for the psychologically strong. For example, issues with expectations, control, intimacy and fear are part of the learning process for all individuals.

Depending on your early development, managing these trials in life can be a positive learning experience or a nightmare. The misery is experienced when you have excessive emotional challenges in the course of everyday life because your sense of self and therefore your thinking is not resilient.

At the core, if you have not received adequate amounts of empathy from the significant people in your life, you become confused as to what behaviors lead to finding love and respect. As your life progresses, not receiving the kind of emotional resonance you needed, it is quite natural to come to the conclusion that you are not "OK." Yet covering this up with a story about what you will achieve, will not make that feeling go away. Doing so gives birth to *Performance Addiction* (PA), an excessive emphasis on appearance and status and all the consequences that come with it.

Your story drives you to the point where you don't manage your energy well, and you become prone to addictive living. An overwhelming feeling and exhaustion then lead to over-stimulating activities like extreme work hours (overachieving), abusing alcohol, poor eating, limited physical inactivity, obesity and other health complications— the "downward trend." This trend undermines all your activity, because a lack of balance and well being dramatically reduces your quality of life. But it does not need to be this way. With objective feedback from the right people, your story can be re-written and you can improve your lifestyle

I have divided the book into four stages so you can see how each aspect of the curse affects the next and how to better resolve lifestyle challenges (how you think and live).

Stage I describes the story you wrote about yourself that was created from compelling yet inaccurate information and why it's not serving you.

Stage II talks about the consequences of your story, *Performance Addiction* and the emotional impact of your fictional story.

Stage III addresses the *six emotional trials of adulthood (expectations, regrets and unfulfilled dreams, control, fear, intimacy, and community)* that are amplified by this addiction and their effect on your thinking.

Stage IV analyzes the compounded distortions in thinking that result from living addictively—the essential concepts we need to heed if any lifestyle solution is going to work in a sustainable way.

The curse is ultimately resolved by developing a new view of you. With objective feedback from the right people your story can be re-written. A more resilient sense of self can emerge with the faith that you can cope with life's challenges. You can thrive while maintaining your overall well-being.

When you begin to identify yourself as someone with this balanced, healthy capability, you will develop the resiliency you need for true success.

I invite you to seek true benefit from this book. It will explain the reasons you were drawn to this book in the first place. Partake in this journey we must all travel to develop an emotionally resilient sense of self!

Let's begin with uncovering your story. We'll look at the thinking that is affecting your current behavior. It is the first step in moving forward to a position of strength, grounded in confidence. Self-awareness is the beginning of the work!

1st Stage—Uncover Your Story

The fictional story you write about yourself.

Your life story comprises the past, the present and your imaginings about your future. What you experience inside and express outwardly to others is quite frankly, "everything" that makes up your self-identity.

The stories you use to describe yourself, especially the internal dialogue, determine your life experience. It doesn't matter if you are telling seemingly positive and optimistic stories to your friends, family and colleagues if internally you are singing a different tune.

For many forward-moving achievers, these stories are a cover-up for how they are genuinely feeling inside. Their inside stories about their lives are not supportive and reflect beliefs and expectations that reinforce negativity, and produce an undesirable life experience.

Achievers tend to mask hardships by trying to be more productive and by extreme accomplishment.

In this stage we're going to explore how the pattern of telling relatively inaccurate, unconstructive or negative stories originated. The following chapters will show you the impact of these inaccuracies and how you can gain freedom from the untruths you have lived with all your life. Ultimately, uncovering the myths of "who you are" is essential to changing your life experience and your lifestyle.

Chapter 1:

The Story You Wrote with a Biased Pen— Your Novel

The nature of your thinking and how you feel about yourself determines how you live.

We are born spirits that soar—light, playful, joyous and blissful. But inevitably, many of us are dragged down by the nitty-gritty of life. We take on roles and responsibilities, overload on stress and worry and crumble beneath the weight of experience and circumstance. By the time we reach adulthood, our personal gravity can become so strong that we can lose sight of our own capacity for happiness and fulfillment. When peace of mind diminishes, we forget what it feels like to feel free; we are overwhelmed with the responsibilities we have assumed and our lifestyle follows suit.

Henry David Thoreau once wrote, "The mass of men lead lives of quiet desperation and go to the grave with the song still in them." I echo this sentiment; it feeds everything I do in my personal and professional life.

Desperation (quiet or otherwise) is the psychological antithesis of liberation. It is born of early experiences that bind our feelings, needs and drives through guilt and shame, thus creating tension and anxiety. This all inhibits the ability to genuinely relate with others and promotes a downward trend in various ways.

These experiences compromise our development and limit healthy relationships with others and ourselves. And the cycle goes around and spirals downward until the story changes or willpower runs out.

Is Your Story Supporting You?

Each of us has a story about ourselves that we have written (so to speak) that defines our experience and for most people defines *who we are*. This story is just that—a story.

For some, this biography is more accurate and positive, based on what actually happened in genuine relationships with others; and from it they learned to interpret events in a constructive way. Even if a particular event is not positive and seemingly negative (as many events in our lives can be), the story created is supportive as it is viewed as a situation in life, not as a self-reflection. This enhances how a person thinks and relates. In other words, bad things can happen and not be a reflection of who we are or what we are worth.

For others, the opposite takes place, and these unfortunate life experiences are interpreted negatively, greatly influencing how a person thinks and relates to others. Because they don't have supportive people helping them to see the difference between situational and personal causes, they create a biased story that does not support a balanced, healthy, high-achieving life.

A positive, self-reinforcing story requires that the key people in our early lives have consistently provided us with *empathy*—the ability to understand and respond to the unique experiences of another. The result of many empathic interchanges is an understanding self-voice. However, if we are not provided with this type of relating, the story written becomes a novel—a fictional story that we use to cope with difficult circumstances.

The Key to a Supportive Story

One of the central themes of this book is the value of being in genuine relationships with others, and for one simple reason: experiencing empathy in relationships with others is the means by which we grow and get to know ourselves.

Empathy is an ability that is absolutely essential in being able to understand others and maneuver through the minefield of relationships. When received, it allows us to form a truthful picture of ourselves, thus being the key component in developing a resilient sense of self.

If empathy was or is still not present in our lives and we are not in authentic relationships with others (and ourselves, for that matter), the likelihood of a fragile sense of self is high. This brings with it emotional challenges, because emotional fitness (which develops in relationships with others) never developed with enough strength to cope effectively.

To compensate for this, we build a cover-up story to relate and appear stronger than we really are which leads to the cultural addiction discussed in the next chapter.

Each chapter in a fictional story about ourselves leads to more inaccuracy and becomes the seeds for low self-esteem, poor self image, errant thinking and perceiving and, inevitably, what you'll come to know as "the downward trend."

The downward trend happens when dynamics like these, lead to negative consequences that accumulate to the point where it becomes progressively more difficult to change course—like a plane going into a downward spiral.

Living overwhelmed leads to exhaustion and fatigue which often result in the overweight condition and health complications. This typically happens emotionally and manifests physically, depending on the circumstances.

The central point of this chapter is this: your story, how you are thinking, is the driving force behind how you live your life. A false or unsupportive story does not serve you, because what is in doubt haunts you and drives you—particularly the unresolved emotional experiences that you cope with by creating more chapters in your novel which reinforce your lifestyle.

The concept of "story" is as powerful as it is because contained within it is the entire idea of identity—your drives, wants, desires, needs, emotional pains, traumas, etc. Even your values, beliefs and rules about life and who you think you are all wrap up nicely in your story.

As a novel, these *character aspects* of your personality don't get fair representation. They become skewed, exaggerated, minimized, repressed and, in some cases, downright denied. All this becomes your shadow, and for many it's a dark shadow. Addiction is born out of this disorder as the need to cover up grows.

Your Story Determines How You Think and Live

Change your story and you can change how you think, feel and live. This can happen in subtle ways every moment of every day as you interpret experiences accurately and positively with exciting and varied outcomes.

To identify your story, listen to yourself speak about anything in your life—about yourself, others, situations, events, your family, past experiences, your health, etc. These are all parts of your story.

What you hear will reveal your values and beliefs, your rules about life, past emotional pains and traumas, needs, wants and desires. Even greater, you'll begin to notice how you've positioned yourself in life and how your experiences are based on those fixed perceptions. In other words, your story is reinforcing the very position you either want to move away from or move toward.

One of my clients, a former professional athlete, uses a simple athletic metaphor to help visualize the process of changing his novel to a non-fiction story. He says it is akin to coaches preparing a team for a football game. The coaches create a story based on assumptions of how the game will be played and won (fiction) beforehand. At halftime, they rewrite the story based on the actual experience of playing the game (the truth,) essentially editing the plan based on actual experience. My client views the process as first-half thinking vs. second-half thinking.

Getting free of your novel story and giving life to a more accurate and joyful view of you, in spite of the seemingly ugly truths you may believe define you, is the purpose of this book. My goal is to help you establish greater peace of mind so you can actually live a balanced, healthy, high-achieving life.

Your Story Determines How You Take Care of Yourself

The reason we achievers tend to not take care of ourselves very well is ultimately based on our stories about *who we are* and *how we are*. Achievement gives us a feeling of control and personal power and seems to deliver the love and respect we all want. Yet, it's easy to understand why there is never enough time and space to take care of ourselves. Given the hectic pace of modern-day life, we can't navigate effectively if we're constantly driven to perform

High achievers in particular don't want to be seen as weak. Meanwhile, nothing will strengthen their sense of self, abilities and capabilities more than having an honest and authentic story about themselves that is relatively balanced and healthy, which they can continually refine and share with others.

The pace of life today is a cultural force that greatly influences our stories and whether or not (and how) we take care of ourselves.

Have you ever noticed your tendency to push on in the face of exhaustion? What aspect of your story drives you to press on that is clearly wearing you down? What needs to change?

Ironically, true strength is the seemingly paradoxical combination of vulnerability and confidence. This combination is attractive because it's honest and authentic. Nobody is perfect (or close to it), and we all have needs that must be met to a reasonable extent—or else we descend into a downward trend. This requires that we acknowledge our needs, which also requires that we reveal our vulnerabilities. We all know this as a basic truth.

Yet those who are driven by an unsupportive story, covering up what seems to be weakness, will drive themselves incessantly until they are forced to stop. Their story reinforces this way of being, and it stems from a fragile sense of self.

You Are Not Alone

Many people have stories based on the dysfunctions of the past caused by a lack of empathic resonance from the important people in their lives and the inevitable fact that they didn't always have access to the support they needed (and many still don't have today). The consequences of this prevent them from forming a true picture of who they are and what they are realistically capable of..

Men in particular (who stereotypically do not express their emotions, or better said, those aspects of their story that are emotional—the truer story) suffer from lack of authentic expression and therefore have greatly biased novels.

Conventionally, women tend to relate with greater emotion and empathy toward one another and therefore experience more authentic expression. This cultural story which reflects our beliefs about women gives them this permission, even though as a gender they are not free of the hidden challenges that make up *the curse*.

Women tend to cover up because of other personal and cultural stories that say they must take care of everyone else first and be the people-pleaser. These gender stereotypes embedded in our culture cause much pain, guilt and tension, as you will see in my client stories throughout this book.

There is value in a great story. Embellishment is part of the human condition and adds spice to life as well as communication. But we must balance the cost of maintaining a story that does not have its roots in an acknowledged reality that is not serving us or those around us.

Your Story: It's What's Driving You

Even if you are famous, it's likely no book has ever been written about YOU. I am not talking about your achievements, but about your true essence.

Remember, our experience of the past is all a story, and our stories represent the many aspects of us listed above (and more). The question is, whether you are relating a novel or a biography to yourself and others. What sense of self do you want to live with? You are in control of the pen.

You can author your story any way you want. But it's best as a biography, not as a novel, and it's best to do so in a way that enables you to live in as balanced and healthy as possible in order to realize your aspirations.

If we don't express our own needs, wants and desires in genuine relationships with others, the disease to please others to make up for what we are not getting becomes rampant. Covered-up emotions lead to heightened sensitivity, and our neediness is hidden but never far behind. It then fuels overachievement for the love and respect we feel we're not getting. Ultimately the story you are creating will determine and form your personality.

A fictional story will create a negative experience. If you have low self-esteem or a poor self image, think for a moment about how this will affect your lifestyle—how you think and live in the process of achieving your goals.

If the internal story you are telling yourself says something like, "I need to be the best, the most, the prettiest, the fittest, etc.," so that you'll gain the love and respect you crave, your lifestyle will likely be unbalanced, perhaps obsessed in a particular area of your life at the great expense of others.

Chances are good you will over or under achieve depending on how you seek the love and respect you want. Underachievers often seek love and respect through sympathy; overachievers seek it through the awe their achievements inspire from others, yet neither way fulfills us. Since achievement in our culture is rewarded so highly, it is no surprise that we choose overachievement more times than not. It has become the story of our culture, but it's also part of the societal cover-up. It is also why addictive living is so rampant.

Your story reflects what's driving you. So if you have unmet needs, wants, desires, covered-up emotions and unresolved issues, look no further than your story to discover why you are thinking and living the way you are.

The Deeper View of Yourself—How Our Stories Emerged

The emotional trials we experience in our lives form the prism through which we remember our past, experience the present and anticipate the future. If that prism is distorted, we lose our ability to accurately view our lives. For example, a person who is unable to resolve the challenge of regret, is more likely to feel pessimistic about the future and less likely to take advantage of opportunities if he or she believes there is a potential for additional regret. Rampant expectations can lead to workaholic tendencies, which can corrode into weak relationships with a spouse, children, or friends.

As we grew up, we looked to the only mirrors we had in our lives, foremost our parents, our siblings, early teachers, coaches and extended family. With each experience, we took account of ourselves. Slowly, but surely, we composed a story, chapter after chapter, based on the ideas we formed about how we believed these important people perceived us.

If our parents' emotional needs went unmet, it's likely our emotional needs went unmet too, particularly in early childhood. In essence we became hardwired in a manner that biased the way we learn about and perceive ourselves, largely through the eyes of others.

We formed deep-seated views of ourselves, partly dependent on the clarity or lack of clarity of others. This is precisely why attractive people believe they are fat and unappealing; intelligent people think they're less than bright; athletic people think they are not gifted; and the beat goes on.

We grow up not realizing that our personal story is partly based on fiction, a novel consisting of ideas about ourselves, created by the biases we absorbed from the people around us. The father who wanted to be the star athlete becomes overly critical of his son's attempts to throw a ball; the mother who wanted to be celebrity beautiful can't help critiquing her young daughter's attire over and over again. The first chapter of our novel reads, "I am less than" and this results in trying "to be more than" which is often where our stories around achievement emerge.

In this *age of achievement*, where the focus on performance is pervasive, if we are operating from a fragile sense of self, performance and achievement become an addiction, a cover-up and futile attempt to get what we long for to feel whole.

They Are, in Part, Paid Forward

We are all born without a sense of self. Our sense of self emerges as we experience the world. Our view of ourselves is created through mirroring. If our parents' needs, feelings and drives were bound by shaming experiences in their own lives, the way they related to us was affected.

Essentially, the guilt and tension was paid forward and passed on (most of the time unconsciously and without any negative intent) by our parents.

Despite the likelihood of their best intentions to do right by us or what's best for us, we were nonetheless looking at a cracked mirror and were getting a distorted view of ourselves.

If we looked in a less dysfunctional mirror, based on healthier relationships early on with empathic communications between people, our perception of ourselves would have been more accurate and clear. But few of us had that luxury.

Our parents had parents too; whatever their experience was, chances are it was passed on to us.

Early on in life we can't see for ourselves, and by the time we can, our eyes are biased so that we can't or don't see objectively. Michael, a client of mine, recently came to a session quite dejected.

He was very disappointed in his fourth flying lesson. "I just messed up the takeoff. I can't regulate the plane the way the instructor taught. It felt humiliating. I couldn't move my feet fast enough or in the right direction."

Now you may be asking, "What's the problem? He's just beginning to learn a new task!" However, if you are suffering from *the curse*, you know exactly what this person is experiencing.

By the way, he is an Ivy League graduate, CEO of his own, very successful company, a former all-state varsity basketball player, recently remarried, has two children by his first wife and lives in an affluent town in Massachusetts. He also owns two other homes in much desired vacation spots in the country. He exercises daily (sometimes twice a day) and could be competitive with any man his age in several sports.

The outer garments are impressive but the inner voice, guided by the novel of his past, holds Michael in a prison. Regardless of what he achieves, he lives with consistent anxiety and misery. The inner pain cannot and will not be cured through external solutions.

Michael comes from a family where both parents had a Budweiser for breakfast along with their coffee and cigarettes. He was the oldest of six children, all pretty much growing up independent of parental supervision. Dad, a decorated Marine, and Mom, the daughter of a local politician, were quite concerned with the image their children presented to the community, but were certainly not hands-on people. They critiqued Michael's basketball performance, but seldom provided any praise, always leaving him with the perception that he had disappointed them in some way.

Michael saw approval when he performed well. He saw disappointment in their mirroring faces when his performance was less than adequate. His sense of self was dependent on the views and perceptions of his parents and other significant people in his life. He became externally driven, not having any sense of what intrinsic direction was like.

All Michael's successes lifted his spirits for a while, but his mood would drop shortly thereafter. Thus, one day, taking a plane lesson for the fourth time, he was filled with criticism and embarrassment. The instructor was probably surprised how seriously he was taking his performance, but if you are dealing with the hidden challenges of *the curse*, you can feel Michael's experience in the marrow of your bones.

You know what it is like to live by a set of standards that can only satisfy temporarily. You live with despair nearly every day of your life, and know that until now, you have likely lost faith in ever discovering how to mend this pain.

Let's Get Real

Coming to grips with your story, the deeper view of yourself and its effects on how you are presently thinking and living is not an easy task, especially when your story about what happened in your life has become so engrained within you.

We believe these stories, both those that are true and those that are false. What we often don't realize is how they are affecting us and driving us to an extreme extent. Our stories become what we think is our personality.

One of the greatest challenges in life is to rewrite your novel and emerge with a new, accurate view of yourself, essentially developing a more resilient personality. Change is possible with the right help and wisdom being imparted to you.

A new client recently asked me, "Is it possible; can I change? I don't believe it can happen, I have been telling myself the same things about myself since I was a kid. How can it possibly change just by sitting in a chair talking to you?"

My answer was, "It won't change just by osmosis. It will change if you have the courage to see yourself more accurately, with help from myself and others. Your resume reads well, we both know that. But for hidden reasons you have felt 'less than' most of your life despite your achievements. You have to trust, over time, that I and the group you are joining will give you a consensus view of yourself that will replace some of the story you have written a long time ago. If you have the courage to engage in this process I can almost guarantee you will change.

Why do I feel so optimistic? Because I can see in your eyes how badly you want to feel free of the negativity that is so much a part of your internal voice. If you can learn to trust me and the others in the group, over time you will begin to hear and incorporate a view of yourself that is likely quite different than the story you have told yourself for years. It may not be a book that is all flattering, but I can assure you it will be a non-fiction story grounded in the reality of who you really are."

My new client seemed emotional as he stood up to leave. He shook my hand firmly and said, "Thanks for having faith. I haven't had much of that in my life." In that moment I could tell he felt alive and had a tinge of hope that what he thought was impossible was in fact, possible. He thought I was giving him my faith, but actually I was giving him the objective truth.

I have spent many years trying to discern what allows people to move toward a more accurate view of themselves and others. The story you write about yourself will affect your life so powerfully that it can realistically be described as the key to happiness and fulfillment.

I am not the first to bring forth this idea of "story," but my aim in pointing out the distinction between a biased, fictional story about you and a true and joyful biography is new. How you uncover your true story is going to make the difference between a life of quiet desperation and one that is liberated.

The core method I have found to be most effective in gaining a more accurate view of yourself is the power of "group," which will be described in detail at various times throughout this book. The power of group consensus cannot be denied, especially when you are part of a group of committed, dedicated people, all in the quest for balance and truth about themselves.

Pen to Paper—Journal Writing with Meaning and Gratitude

Several studies over recent years have established the psychological and physical benefits of keeping a journal for personal growth reasons.

People who have suffered from trauma have improved their health and well-being by writing about their experiences.

Putting pen to paper has proven to be healing in terms of releasing emotion and gaining insight.

A few years ago psychology professor, James Pennebacker of Southern Methodist University, demonstrated that journal writing improves immune function, liver enzyme function and enhances overall health due to the emotional release of unburdening oneself.

Dr. Pennebacker encouraged participants in his studies to find meaning in their narrative stories. Essentially, his instruction was to find meaning in difficulties rather than letting situations produce lasting negativity.

Most interesting in this regard is the work of Dr. Robert Emmons, psychologist and researcher in the area of the science of gratitude. In his book *Thanks: How the New Science of Gratitude Can Make You Hap-*

pier, he cites studies that he and colleagues conducted on the effects of a daily gratitude journal. In his experimental studies, persons who were randomly assigned to keep gratitude journals on a weekly basis exercised more regularly, were more optimistic and had fewer unhealthy physical symptoms than those individuals who simply recorded hassles in their lives.

In a further study he conducted, young adults keeping a gratitude journal reported higher levels of alertness, determination, energy and enthusiasm compared to a group whose journals were focused on stressors and ways in which they thought they were better off than others. An unexpected finding of gratitude journaling was that people felt closer and more connected to others. They were more likely to demonstrate empathy to those around them while expanding their social network with mutually satisfying, reciprocal relationships.

In essence, journal writing focused on finding meaning in our stories with the accompanied feeling of gratitude was both productive and healing. Please keep a journal based on the questions I ask at the end of each chapter and, as a result, questions will emerge to be explored further.

Remember the research cited above and try to focus on deriving meaning from your answers, while exhibiting gratitude for being in this worthwhile process. I think this exercise will prove fruitful for you. If you'd like to, you may choose to share your responses on our blog and in our ongoing discussion forums.

Questions to Journal:

Download your free journal at:
www.TheCurseoftheCapable.com/ChangeYourStory so you can track
your responses to journal questions througout the book with ease.

The following are the first set of questions to answer. They are designed to help you explore your story and begin the process of rewriting your biography. I encourage you to write in the spaces after each
question and record your answers spontaneously, then get grounded in
experience by taking the steps that follow the questions.

- What are the first thoughts that come to mind when you think of
  your story?

- Who are the most influential people who have shaped your story?

- Did any of these people have the capacity to accurately perceive
  who you are? Explain.

- What are his/her shortcomings in perception?

- What are the most impressionable hurts you recorded in your
  childhood?

- How have those hurts shaped your story?

- What feedback do you currently receive from credible sources
  that you can't seem to integrate into your view of yourself?

- What do you think are the reasons you hold on so tightly to your
  story?

- What threatens you in terms of integrating new information
  about your personality?

- Do you realize that one way of holding on to people in your past
  is to continue to adopt their view of you? How can you change
  this pattern?

- What are the risks in those relationships if you change your fictionalized story?

Get Grounded in Experience:

1. Ask a very close friend what aspect of your story he or she thinks is a distortion.

2. Commit to behaving in a way this week that will alter your distorted view. For instance, if you are hesitant to ask questions at a staff meeting because your story says you're not very intelligent, try to ask a question or make a comment at the very moment the old self-doubt emerges. Take action on whatever aspect of your story your friend brought into question.

2nd Stage—Discover the Consequences of Your Story

The resulting syndrome that may be ruining your life—Performance Addiction (PA); it's what happens if the story you write with a biased pen does not change.

Discovering the behaviors that your stories have prompted is the next phase of gaining freedom. When you can see the connection between the stories you tell and your behaviors, you can then affect change.

Understanding the effects of Performance Addiction will help you gain awareness of how this syndrome leads to heightened and often negative emotions as well as the overspending of vital energy. The most identifiable aspect of *the curse*, energy depletion, is a prominent result of Performance Addiction. Energy gain is the consistent benefit of addressing this syndrome and learning in your heart and in your head what truly brings love and respect.

Chapter 2:
How to Achieve for the Right Reasons— Performance Addiction

Thousands of capable, high-achieving people are suffering from Performance Addiction (PA), which is the belief that perfecting appearance and achieving status will secure love, respect and happiness. It is born out of an unsupportive story about the past. PA is the most common characteristic of *the curse* given the reinforcement of non-stop performance in today's day and age. It is an irrational, inaccurate belief system, hardwired from earlier experiences, reinforced by cultural expectations. It is often rewarded and usually leads to over-doing and overachievement.

Performance addicts turn to activity like alcoholics turn to a drink and like gamblers are drawn to the gambling table. If performance addicts are not constantly busy achieving something, they don't feel worthy. When good performance doesn't buy them happiness, they think they must perform even better. When that effort fails, they decide to try harder, go faster, be more dedicated and ultimately they believe they must make more sacrifices.

Performance addicts believe in the religion of perfection. They think they can perfect their way into happiness. As a result, they can end up achieving their goals for the wrong reasons; this usually takes their life terribly off course. The emotional consequences of this are also experienced physically, as this all takes an immense amount of personal energy. As their energy gets low without recuperation, they can go into a downward energy trend that is equally challenging to acknowledge and change.

The overwhelming feeling created by the emotional drive to perform, particularly at something they don't really enjoy, leads to exhaustion and fatigue.

The Downward Trend

An addiction to performance, regardless of the underlying reasons, requires that you stimulate your way through the day to keep going.

The methods employed are usually more food, stimulants and yes, more activity.

Even if the "stimulant" is exercise, the body gets more exhausted because of a lack of recovery. Facing a true exhaustive state without a feeling of accomplishment (which those with PA have difficulty experiencing because they are always on to the next thing) is depressing and persistent.

The downward trend continues; the psychological pattern of PA now becomes an energy drain with physical manifestations. Rarely if ever stepping back to change the pattern, the addicted person presses on for elusively better results in his body, his life and his business.

He or she seeks quicker, more effective solutions—fitness programs, diets and drug fixes—to deal with the ever-present health problems such as fatigue and weight gain.

But this can only be solved by stepping back and changing your lifestyle and essentially how you achieve your goals in the world. As the symptoms of this pattern are suppressed en masse, we get an emerging population of increasingly more anxious performance addicts with seemingly less time, energy and space to take care of themselves. This could describe our culture.

When sharing the title for this book with others prior to publishing, no sooner would I get the words out of my mouth when someone would say something to the effect of "Whatever it is, I've got it" or "I know what you're talking about."

Anyone who has followed the path of dealing with symptoms, but avoided the roots of the problem, knows in his or her heart it does not work. Health statistics are the perfect example; they get worse and worse as obesity climbs up 6% per year.

The "quick fix" (from the top down or outside in) for what are really lifestyle issues (that require a bottom up or from the inside out solution), is anything but quick. It seems to work in the short term, but in the end the gain is usually outweighed by the pain of compounding problems still covered up.

The downward trend creates misery and potentially a "lost cause" outlook as the roots of PA, its psychological challenges and physical consequences are buried deep and out of sight. You know you need to change, but like all addictions, tomorrow your defense of rationalization and your "second wind" takes over. You return to using the only methods you know work; at least you know they work temporarily.

In our society we know that if you look good and also have credentials and money (despite an unhealthy lifestyle,) you are going to be idealized for a while; but if these results are based on an addiction to performance and a poor lifestyle, it's only a matter of time before the curse takes its destructive toll. It was this realization that originally inspired *The Curse of the Capable*.

The addiction itself is not the cause; you have to uncover the root causes if you really want to solve the problem and stay off the downward trend.

The quest for relief typically starts with a recommitment to goals, higher levels of activity and productivity, a new exercise program, a stricter diet regimen, more attempts to please others etc. to deal with the symptoms of this driven, yet overwhelming and exhausting way of life that can leave you feeling helpless despite your obvious capabilities. Unfortunately, none of those efforts deal with the hidden challenges or its roots, which will magnify during periods of stress. Irrational and inaccurate belief systems emotionally hardwired from earlier experiences drive us in self-destructive ways, even though the actions may appear admirable.

In a world where performance is rewarded to maintain productivity and quick fixes are the norm, performance addicts are at an extreme disadvantage. Amidst the cultural expectations for achievement, they are unable to assert their personal preferences, set boundaries or take care of themselves at the level they need to maintain balance, health and well-being. They may be achieving their goals, but living out of balance, they are trading their health to do it. Once you are on this downward trend, all aspects of *the curse* are amplified.

Discovering PA

Since the publication of *Performance Addiction; the Dangerous New Syndrome and How to Stop it from Ruining Your Life* in 2004, I have had numerous referrals from very bright, engaging people suffering from PA. It has surprised me that people will drive over two hours from neighboring states to talk about their never-ending attempts to balance their lives.

I mention this fact, not from an inflated ego position, but to indicate how desperate PA victims become, how miserable their internal lives can be despite every outward indication to the contrary and how determined they are to gain relief.

Anthony, an entrepreneur from Rhode Island, comes every Friday with a look of stress written all over his face. He is handsome, holds an MBA from a prestigious college, is married with three daughters, and has attained a level of financial success anyone would envy. He owns two homes; his extended family members are all alive and are quite connected through seeing and talking with each other frequently. His children are healthy and his wife loves him very much.

Yet, despite the impressive resume, he is miserable!

You Look Marvelous, but…

What keeps Anthony from living up to his resume? His father and older brother are both attorneys and his youngest sister is an executive in the clothing business. They grew up in an affluent town in Southeast Rhode Island and he was expected to be like his older brother —handsome, athletic and charming.

When Anthony entered high school his brother left for college. He was immediately reminded by coaches and teachers of his brother's academic achievements and of his athletic prowess.

His father, now a professor at a local law school, placed great emphasis on his childrens' achievements. Both parents, being Italian American, also placed great emphasis on family involvement.

Sunday dinner was a ritual at their grandmother's house, with everything and anything open for discussion. Dating a girl from another less prestigious town was frowned upon; and not wearing the right clothes or speaking with improper grammar was an imperfection to be immediately corrected. Regardless of who was present or in what situation they were, the talk was frank, direct, never compromising and shameless.

Anthony's father was super critical of his "uneducated wife." She tried valiantly to please him, but never won the battle. She didn't speak correctly and dressed "like an old lady." The complaints went on and on as the children listened.

When Anthony was in graduate school, his father had an affair. He left school for a semester to care for his mother, as she fell into a deep depression. Anthony, unfortunately, learned to identify with his mother while fearing his father.

The Making of Anxiety

Anthony learned early in life that appearance and status were crucial to being loved. This is the precise, shame-based formula that creates an anxious person and also develops the curse.

As he listened to his mother's torment, Anthony discovered his mother felt she was not good enough to keep her husband from straying. No matter how hard she tried to protect her son and hold her husband accountable, Anthony knew in her heart she blamed herself.

If only she had kept her figure; if only she had taken some courses as her husband had instructed; if only she could have become different, more sexy, less inhibited; and so on. He internalized her belief system that said, "You're only loved as long as you look good and maintain a certain status in the world."

Anthony became an anxious person, always worrying about his performance and how he compared to others. In high school his coaches would say, "You're a great practice player; why can't you perform like this in a game?" The answer was obvious, he told me one night, "My father didn't watch practices but the moment I saw him enter the park on the day of a game, my heart would start beating."

Despite this pressure he still managed to become an all-state quarterback and a star baseball player. "But I knew I was never playing as well as I could. My senior year I got hurt, tore up my shoulder and I was secretly grateful that I had a good reason to escape the pressure." He went on to say that he never told anyone how relieved he was to be hurt, having an escape from what he considered to be an emotional prison.

Anthony stumbled into college, drank too much, prayed for a way out of his athletic scholarship, but continued to do what he thought would be acceptable to his father and most other authority figures.

He dated but never allowed himself to get too close. Women liked him because he was unusually respectful and sensitive to females (because his mother was the one soothing person in his life.) He knew his mother understood him, but he was afraid to be with her for too long, because she was prone to low moods. In his words, her moods "were catchy."

He found himself attracted to women who depended on him, women who would quickly let him know he was liked and that they needed him. These relationships became burdensome; he would find some reason to disengage but always with an unusual level of guilt.

Eventually in graduate school he met and married his wife Paula, a pretty woman who is quite dependent and often overwhelmed in her role as a mother. Anthony works in his business, often does the food shopping and cooks most nights despite his long hours away from home.

He loves his children but has much trouble setting limits with them, usually finding their tears and tantrums unbearable. "I can't stand to see them upset. I just give in to stop my own anxiety. I know it's wrong, but when they are emotional I fall apart."

Paula complains about Anthony drinking and eating too much. She feels rejected by his tendency to want to be alone. He still works out, is somewhat obsessed with his physique and spends time reading muscle books to recapture the "body I had in college."

Despite all these dynamics, Anthony is a person of integrity and high ethics. He is well-liked in business and although he seldom reaches out to friends, he is someone in whom people confide with. He is known to be dependable in a crisis. All these abilities are matched by an equal amount of anxiety and unhappiness.

Can I Change or Is It Too Late?

Anthony had reached out for help with his primary care physician after weeks of poor sleep and worry. He was referred to a psychiatrist and placed on Prozac for depression and Ativan for anxiety. He felt some relief in the early weeks and would meet with his doctor every so often to talk about the medication and occasional adjustments to the dosage. The short term gain eroded over time and one night he Googled the word *perfection* and stumbled onto my second book, *Performance Addiction*. It took him several weeks to make the call, but we eventually met and continued working on his PA in individual sessions.

Ultimately, Anthony joined one of my weekly group-coaching sessions and he continues attending today. He has made remarkable strides as his internal story has changed and he has become more emotionally resilient; not perfect strides, but nevertheless remarkable. He is more relaxed, more able to be intimate with his wife, more able to tolerate the emotions of three young girls and more able to view his work and his appearance in a realistic framework.

I don't mean to convey that his life is always in order, for it is not. Does he have times when he resorts to old ways of coping? Yes. Does he occasionally doubt himself as he has in the past? Yes. Does he, on occasions, withdraw from his wife instead of speaking and addressing conflict? Yes.

But the difference today is that the old behaviors are truly old, like old records he can turn off as soon as he recognizes self-defeating patterns. In essence, the old hardwiring has been altered and new wiring has been created. There are still memories of certain behavioral patterns but new neurons, new brain chemistry and new enriched pathways of behavior have replaced them; the new aspects of Anthony's brain overpowers the old.

The Ultimate Transformation

How did these fundamental changes happen? They took place in the interpersonal world. The nature of our experiences in relationship with others has the potential to change our brains. High quality interactions can and will allow us to make permanent change for the better, and on a neurochemical level.

We are bombarded in the media by pharmaceutical advertising. We are told we can change the nature of our brains through certain medications.

The method I am advocating in this book is more powerful and more permanent than any pharmaceutical change can ever produce.

I am not anti-medication; I am simply judicious regarding their use. In our culture we have become quite lax in terms of thoughtfully examining the purpose and use of anti-depressants, anti-anxiety drugs and the like.

One fact supported by neuroscientists around the world is enormously encouraging: we can change the way we perceive and the way we feel about ourselves which ultimately causes neurochemical changes that make us healthier, more vibrant and alive; enabling us to think and live better.

In Anthony's case, our relationship gave him a new perspective regarding the possibilities that can occur between people. Oftentimes he would return the next week and say he knew he felt better when he left a session, but he wasn't always sure exactly what happened.

One day, Anthony revealed to me, "I think I have been feeling more comfortable in my own skin. For the first time in my life I feel understood; I am more accepting of myself. I guess it's because I think you accept and know me. I don't think you agree with everything I say, but when you give me feedback, even if it's not complimentary, I don't worry about your intent. I know you're trying to help me.

If your words hurt, I've come to realize they are words I need to hear in order to move forward in my life."

True happiness (love and respect, health and well-being) and personal and professional success comes when people have developed strong relationship skills, especially the capacity for *empathy* and lifestyles that promote sustainability.

Performance addicts tend to rate status over character, achievement over relationships and productivity over healthy performance levels.

The result of their drive to achieve is to cover up vulnerability. They only recover when they learn in their hearts and in their heads that successful living begins with relationships. Interpersonal skills are indispensable to gaining what has been missing all their lives.

You may be wondering why "relationships," "interpersonal skills," and "empathy" are the primary solution to the problem. The ability to relate and communicate with others is necessary for every aspect of personal growth and development; relationships are the mirrors necessary to learning about ourselves. They help us face denied aspects of ourselves that we suppress or are unable to acknowledge.

For the performance addict, it is essential to strengthen the underlying and fragile sense of self if thinking and living better is going to be possible, let alone sustainable, free of the compulsive and obsessive drives to keep performing. This requires a little help from your friends. It requires genuine perspective.

You can be aware of "work life" balance and have a PhD in nutrition and exercise, but if you are emotionally hardwired to incessantly perform for the wrong reasons, you'll be constantly challenged.

A resilient and optimistic sense of self can only be developed interpersonally. Reading self help books may help, but the solution is in developing empathic interpersonal skills in relationships with others in a group or community.

With a stronger and clearer sense of self developed with others with similar goals, how you think and live improves as you get free of the irrational drives that keep you performing (ruminating, comparing, obsessing, proving etc.) all the time. With appropriate feedback from others, you are likely to develop more genuine relating, especially if those around you are committed to truthful interchanges. When this is so, an emotionally fit and resilient sense of self develops.

Numerous studies have indicated that interpersonal skills are fundamental to success in diverse career paths. In the corporate world, successful executives have the ability to "sense others' needs" and to "make others feel heard." They don't always agree with their employees but they attend to their employees. Essentially these executives have developed the capacity for empathy—the ability to understand and respond to the unique experiences of another.

Sounds like a formula for good parenting too, doesn't it?

Understanding the Unique Experiences of Another

Anthony was not accustomed to being listened to without judgment or fear of criticism, from his father in particular.

Over the past few years I have realized that PA victims not only suffer from anxiety regarding their appearance and status, they are also people who generally are anxious in the presence of others. Many don't show this vulnerability, for they have learned effective ways to mask their fear.

I have worked with many clients who could deliver a speech while seemingly confident and at ease. But inside they were constantly scanning the audience in fear of spotting a person who looked bored or disapproving.

Often this manifests as a low level anxiety that is always present, so that a person accommodates to this state of mind like a person who gets accustomed to a low energy level without realizing she is burnt out. Anthony, for instance, knew he always lived with a level of tension inside, but just assumed this was his makeup and was not likely to change.

His perspective changed as he participated in group sessions over a period of weeks. In his initial session he was anxious, as should be expected. However, he thought this was unusual, thinking other people probably coped better on their first try (a story he told himself.) Everyone smiled when he made a comment to this effect. They smiled because they all felt the same way when they began, and in each case they came to realize how little they understood about the human condition.

Human beings often have anxiety when they try something new, especially when it involves revealing their true nature. PA robs individuals of actually coming to understand what people tend to experience in any significant circumstance.

The PA sufferer's preoccupation with their own performance deprives them of really seeing and understanding how other people actually feel. They are often rehearsing what to say rather than truly listening, again losing the opportunity to learn and observe. Their tendency to idealize is strong, as is the wish to excel. The belief that perfection actually exists drives them to do more and try harder. Ultimately, this process leads to the loss of energy and low mood, as each attempt at perfection usually results in that feeling of helplessness.

Beyond Inadequacy

PA drives a person to long to be great, to overcompensate for feelings of inadequacy. They experience a constant tension between these two extremes, most often not realizing the truth lies somewhere in the middle. PA's are not as great as they want to be, but conversely are not as bad as they think they are (even though this is not about the duality of "good or bad" which alone can cause distorted thinking.)

Once this dilemma is understood, the work is to change inadequate feelings, assessing whether they are based in truth or are part of a story they have written in their minds over the years that prompt old emotional states.

Slowly but surely, Anthony became liberated from his condition as he came to realize from the truthful feedback of group members and myself what is myth and what is accurate about himself. He essentially dropped the weight of his past so that he could feel free once again, unencumbered by the false notions that had burdened him.

It is not an easy to have the courage to face yourself. We all have our shortcomings and our strengths but perfectionists have little tolerance for weakness. Still we all carry the memory of painful past experiences. Unfortunately for many, particularly those suffering from PA, these past experiences have become their identity.

Traumatic past experiences or significant emotional hurts usually stay that way in the mind. We maintain a fixed image of ourselves that was a consequence of the story our emotional pain created. This recording can change when someone is in a group of his or her peers, where he or she reveals his or her vulnerabilities and strengths to obtain a deeper, more accurate view of him or her self. This ultimately reveals a new, more understanding and considerate story.

We cannot arrive at self-knowledge without the participation of others, along with the reciprocal use of empathy. The *power of empathy* is in creating intimacy, self-understanding, and lasting love. A book by this title (my first book) is the other recommended read to help you grasp the essential skill required to get free of *the curse* and its challenges. This will be experienced in the group process I refer to throughout this book.

It is quite likely that most people in our culture are performance addicts to a certain degree. There are healthy levels of comparison and competitiveness. It's when achievement becomes your method of coping with the vulnerabilities of your past that performance addiction can rule your life.

Questions to Journal:

If you haven't already downloaded your free journal go to: www.TheCurseoftheCapable.com/ChangeYourStory.

Now I encourage you to take out your pen and answer the following questions in the space provided, or record in a separate journal that you'll use alongside this book.

- What part of Anthony's story do you identify?

- Does his life story cause any particular emotional reaction in you?

- Did you experience one or both of your parents as critical people in general?

- Do you have memories of specific childhood hurts that never left you?

- Were you easily humiliated as a young person?

- Do you always have a to-do list in your mind or in your pocket?

- Do you often feel you have to work much harder than others to excel? Why?

- Did you worry that if you didn't please your parents you would lose their love?

- Are you frequently trying to perfect the way you speak?

- Are you frequently trying to perfect your appearance?

- Are you unable to stop perfectionist thinking even though you know it's irrational?

- Do you feel guilty if you hang out and do nothing?

- Do you question whether you have true friends?

- Do you weigh yourself daily?

- Are you intolerant of the aging process?

- Do you measure success without giving much weight to a person's character?

- Do you exercise too little or too much?

- Are you on a diet at least once a year?

- Do you use alcohol, drugs or comfort foods in excess to calm down?

- Do you take sleep aids daily or monthly?

- Can you explain the "yes" answers to the above questions?

Get Grounded In Experience:

1. Record in your journal the most enjoyable moments of your week. How many of those moments involved status and appearance?

2. Choose an activity that does not involve performance, one that you enjoy but would not consider "being productive," and try to enjoy the experience as much as possible without self-criticism.

3rd Stage—Acknowledge the Emotional Impact of Your Story: The 6 Trials of Adulthood.

The six universal emotional trials that are heightened by Performance Addiction, their effect on your behavior and the story you are telling that reinforces your view of yourself.

In this stage, you will hear the stories of my clients who have struggled with the six emotional challenges all adults must face and work through to be successful. I have learned over many years that these are struggles we all face. They are especially influential in the life of the high achiever. You will come to understand how each of these emotional trials is resolved and how intimately related your story is to how you cope.

We get attached to people and situations that support and continue our unique stories. Our deepest view of our self is reflected in these choices and the way we decide to cope with the challenges we encounter. The following chapters display how old, misguided views of our self, (an unconstructive story) prevent constructive coping. As these patterns are altered, energy is unleashed to address life's difficulties. A new view of "you" creates an energy reserve that puts you in a position of strength to successfully deal with new situations.

Chapter 3:
A Chemical High—
Expectations

Controlled by the Numbers

When Sara first came to my office three years ago, she was a walking example of a woman held hostage by her expectations. At 5'2" and quite slight of build, she was used to slipping into rooms unnoticed—unpretentious, ordinary, entirely forgettable. She looked timid, even fragile. An undercurrent of tension made her casual blue jeans, baggy shirt and multi-colored hair seem like a false study in "cool". She collapsed in the corner of the couch as if the mere act of sitting defeated her.

Through our discussions, I learned that, despite her less-than-extraordinary persona, Sara was a world-class singer who had played with many jazz musicians of note and was critically acclaimed internationally.

As she told me about her life, I remember thinking there was nothing lyrical about her. I found myself wondering why she wasn't breezier, mellower and lighter—anything but the leaden personality digging her fingernails into my upholstery.

After a few sessions, the answer revealed itself: Sara was in the process of turning away from music. Despite a life defined by her art, she had lost that feeling of joy and satisfaction.

Sara experienced new offers to sing as unwanted pressure, but simultaneously, incongruously, feared that each performance would be the last, so she took them all and hated herself for doing it. She worried about singing in public, wary of the "judgmental eyes" that stared at her during concerts.

Instead of enjoying her talent and reveling in her enviable level of success, Sara felt tapped out and was considering quitting the career she had worked so hard to build. In a very real way, the music had drained out of her.

It can take much hard psychological work to unravel how people lose their claim to a liberated life and adopt *the curse*, but Sara's core issue was easier to identify than most. She had become a victim of that epidemic and toxic form of expectation I call the *numbers*.

Keeping Score of Your Life

The human mind naturally seeks out ways to gauge success or failure. Even very young children instinctively watch adults for signs of approval and adapt their behavior to elicit more, bigger, stronger responses. They can process nuances of expression faster than the time it takes to realize you've made a grave error in judgment.

For example, if you chuckle the first time your toddler shows off his ability to burp, you will create a burping machine that will be nearly impossible to turn off—if his trick worked to make you happy once, the deepest level of his brain will be convinced that it will work again, so he will repeat the burp once...twice...ten times, day after day. You'll become exhausted of listening to the belches long before the child tires of trying to please you. You know the phrase "Don't laugh—it just encourages him"? It was coined to cover this particular psychological phenomenon.

We never really lose the urge to *win* approval, or more simply, to win. But our measures of success change. Through observation, family indoctrination, social values and personal goals, we internalize certain standards of performance. These become our expectations. In our society, we are fascinated with competition and benchmarks. And the most surefire way to ensure accuracy in measurement is to attach a number to it.

They are ubiquitous, these *numbers* of our expectations. They are the scores we want on SATs, the age by which we fear we will die, the salary we think we deserve, the size of our 401K, the number of Web pages returned when we Google our own names, the square footage of our homes, the length of our vacations, our weight, breast size, credit rating, and on and on. Almost any achievement can be expressed as a number.

Try this experiment—the next time you meet someone, ask if they are married. If the answer is yes, more often than not, it will be followed by a number, as in, "Yes, for eight years." It is difficult to reduce a relationship to a number, but we still manage to do it. And if we can quantify marriage, everything else is easy.

There are precious few aspects of our world that we do not count, measure or compare. For better or worse, these *numbers* are the yardsticks by which we judge our success or failure as we move through life.

Of course, *the numbers* don't *really* tell us anything about success or failure. At most, they are a snapshot of our values at a given time, and about the values of our parents, who helped to instill some of our love of setting goals and meeting expectations.

There is nothing inherently wrong with having goals or striving to achieve them—that's how we reach our potential and find fulfillment. The problem comes when we confuse abstract, ultimately meaningless numbers as the true goals, or if we exaggerate their importance or use them as a cover for some fragility in our personality. In those situations, we are no longer in control; instead, we become hostage to those deceptive expectations.

As we desperately try to "make the numbers," we become locked in a cycle of negative emotions and futile behaviors, all while looking to *the numbers* for clues as to how we are doing, how we should be feeling and whether our lives are on the right track.

It sounds extreme, but we all fall for it from time to time, especially those stricken with PA. Think about stepping on a scale to check your weight. If you are like most people, you remember what your weight was the previous time you measured. That number is your weight expectation.

What if you weighed yourself today and discovered you were ten pounds lighter than you thought you were—how would you feel? I'm guessing you would be elated. If you discovered instead that you had gained ten pounds, you would probably feel distressed.

Your expectation has the power to shift your emotions in an instant, based solely on the interaction between the number on the scale and the number in your head. The number is your benchmark. Any change in circumstance that is better than your benchmark will tend to make you happier; in the same way, any change that is worse than the benchmark can drain happiness.

This works similarly for just about anything. If you expect a raise of $50 per week, finding out that you will actually get an extra $100 per week will probably thrill you; but a raise of only $10 per week will likely make you angry. In a very real way, numbers have the power to alter our emotional life—for better or worse.

Better Than, Worse Than

Depending on the meaning an individual places on a number, the results of failing to meet this arbitrary goal can be devastating. As a singer, Sara had set the bar for her success pretty high. Singers have to be darn **good** for people to pay to hear them and they have to be **excellent** to make a living at it. To be associated with stars and acclaimed on three continents, they have to be great. But Sara didn't recognize those markers as meaningful. Instead, she fell prey to that peculiar phenomenon common among musicians and singers (and for that matter writers)—the *Amazon obsession*, an ideal manifestation of performance addiction.

Anyone who has ever spent time browsing the *amazon.com* website knows that individual CDs, books, and other merchandise are ranked according to their *amazon.com* sales. The number-one, best-selling CD is given a sales rank of #1, the number-five best-selling CD has a sales rank of #5, and so on (well into the millions). The rankings are updated frequently—hourly for items ranked #1 through #999, daily for those ranked lower.

Sara's newest CD had debuted at #798, which is respectable, but it wouldn't get her on any lists of top-selling jazz CDs. When she checked again the next day, the CD rank had improved to #336. An hour later, it was at #421. An hour after that, #487...#222...#159...#898...obsession *ad infinitum.* Sara checked the ranking every hour or so for the next five days, hoping to see validation of her efforts—which she defined as reaching the top 10. Despite heroic publicity efforts, it never happened. That is when Sara started to spiral into a *numbers* panic.

After about a week of watching her CD's ranking skip up and down the charts, Sara decided to track the CDs of other singers she knew. She chose some singers she respected and liked and others she thought were overrated or dull. Every day she compared her ranking to those of the other artists and every day she found new reason to hate her profession.

If a good singer's CD ranked higher than hers, Sara would become despondent, hopeless because she felt she would never achieve the same level of seemingly effortless talent. If an undeserving singer (in Sara's humble opinion) had a CD with a better ranking than hers, Sara would howl at the unjust nature of fame. When Sara's ranking reached about #100,000 (as most eventually do), her expectations were well shattered, leaving Sara feeling lost, depressed and anxious. In her own eyes, she was a loser.

Expectations drive desire and hope, but expecting to correct an emotional deficit with a positive accomplishment leads ultimately to depression. Expectations are caused by a natural yearning to actualize one's potential and, on a deeper level, a conditioned belief as to what behaviors or accomplishments will bring love and boost our sense of self.

Our expectations dramatically affect our neurochemistry, producing the feel-good chemical dopamine. Neuroscientists call this "expectation anticipation." The anticipation releases dopamine before the actual goal is reached. Sara is a great example. She has a natural talent she longed to develop, an uncanny ability to sing and play music. She often gets high in anticipation of how well her next recording will do on the charts.

Sara is a perfectionist, as many high achievers are, but not all perfectionism has negative consequences. Research on this topic has displayed two types of perfectionism. The healthy form is exhibited in individuals who have extraordinary abilities and like to live up to their potential. They are not primarily performing to gain others' love; the love they receive comes as a by-product of the passion they have for their vocation.

The second form of perfectionism is trying, in Sara's case, to rewrite the novel she has written in her head since her childhood by becoming the best singer/songwriter in the country. Her drive is to change her negative self-view by being "the best"— someone one who will supposedly be envied by all. Ironically, human beings, as research has confirmed over and over again, are incredibly inaccurate as to what achievements will actually bring lasting satisfaction.

People Are Not Like Rats (Usually)

The *Amazon obsession* is a recent phenomenon, but it has precedence in several psychological theories, including reward theories. Take classic *operant conditioning*, which is based on the observation that behavior that is rewarded tends to be repeated (i.e. if you reward a toddler with a laugh when he burps, he'll burp as often as possible to try to get you to laugh again.)

Early versions of this theory proposed that all human behavior could be predicted if we knew the pattern of rewards and punishments each person received throughout his or her life.

When laboratory rats were taught to press levers to win food pellets, operant conditioning was a perfectly fine and workable theory. But in other contexts, it doesn't work so well. Consider this scenario: You have two rooms full of kindergarten students who are drawing with crayons. The children in the first room are left to draw on their own. The children in the second room are told that they will receive a dollar for every drawing they turn in to the teacher. The next week, you return to see how the children are doing. What do you suppose would happen?

Most people guess that the children who were promised a dollar per drawing would have a stack of finished artwork and be working furiously to create more, while the other group of children would be less productive. Indeed, that's what operant conditioning would predict—getting rewarded with money should motivate the children to make more artwork.

But in fact, when this study was done in the real world, the exact opposite happened. The children who were offered money to do what they already loved eventually lost interest in the activity. There was an initial flurry of drawing, but it dwindled to almost nothing, while the unrewarded children continued to draw.

It turns out that people are more complicated than rats pressing a lever. Go figure. People—as opposed to lab rats—have complex personalities, self-determination and other internally driven factors that directly affect our personal growth and well-being. One of the most powerful of those factors is motivation.

Motivating Forces

Motivation is part inspiration—the reasons we do what we do. Psychologists separate motivation into two main categories: intrinsic and extrinsic.

Intrinsic motivation is real, authentic motivation that comes from within the individual. People with intrinsic motivation have a natural interest in a topic or action, and do what they do for the sheer joy of it. This interest breeds excitement, energy and creativity, which in turn, feed the motivation like a perpetual motion machine.

People with intrinsic motivation will continue to pursue their interests even if they never receive recognition or monetary gain or long after they "have to" continue working. For example, Tony Bennett was recently asked why, at age 85, he continues to sing. His answer was simple: "Because I love it."

Extrinsic motivation comes from outside the individual and can include rewards, threats or goals imposed by others. It is the reason we do things that are unpleasant or that we have no interest in. It is one of the symptoms consistent with PA. Extrinsic motivation explains why people continue to work at jobs they hate (money is a common external reward) or why the threat of grounding can keep some teens from staying out past curfew. If extrinsic motivation is the only thing guiding behavior, then people will stop acting as soon as the reward or threat is removed.

Sounds simple, right? Internal or external, and never any confusion; well, psychologists discovered an interesting twist to the motivation story. It turns out that it is remarkably easy to kill intrinsic motivation so that a natural interest shrivels and dies. All you have to do is apply tangible rewards, threats, or other external pressure. That's what happened with the kindergarten children who were paid to draw.

Kids naturally love to create artwork, which means that they have intrinsic motivation. The payment of a dollar per drawing dampened that natural enthusiasm by imposing an external reward. That outside interference—even though it was something good and valuable—transformed a loved activity into a tedious chore, motivation gone! That spark of human spirit was snuffed.

This is also what happened to Sara. She did not become a singer because her parents forced her to or because it was a high-paying job—in fact, there were quite a few lean years before Sara was able to support herself. Rather, Sara's natural love of jazz and music drove her choice of activity and career.

When she was young and inspired from within, she would have continued playing even if she had to wait tables to make ends meet. But she was talented, lucky and motivated (intrinsically). She was able to overcome the odds and become a successful singer and musician.

Her tripping point was the *Amazon obsession*. When Sara started watching her sales rank, she introduced her own outside interference— the pressure to have her CD meet her performance expectations, to meet her *number*. That was enough to dampen her motivation. Over time, Sara lost the joy of her music. By the time she came to see me, Sara was talking about abandoning singing for good.

Trading Up the Number

The numbers can take many forms. They can be test scores, weight, quo-
tas at work, or just about anything you can imagine. The human mind
is adept at creating new standards to try to meet. The most common
number category is money—how much we make per year, how much
we have in the bank, how much we spend on shoes, how much richer we
are than our brothers-in-law. I have nothing against making or having
money—I enjoy a paycheck as much as the next guy—and in general, it
is not a negative influence. However, our *expectations* about money, the
numbers we attach to it, can strongly affect our level of happiness.

Take Joanna, a client who is fixated on the number 250,000—dollars,
that is. She is a marketing director at a large manufacturing corporation.
When she began her career 15 years ago, she thought making $100,000
per year would be proof that she had made it in the business world—the
idea of making "six figures" was a status she had aspired to since she was
in college. She achieved that number within three years. It was satisfying,
but the happiness she felt was temporary.

Almost immediately, she replaced that number with a new one—
$150,000. This pattern repeated until she found a number she couldn't
crack. According to Joanna, all the "real talent" (her words) in her company made $250,000 per year. If she could make that quarter-million,
then she would know that she was of the same caliber. Of course, if she
does end up making her number, the satisfaction will be transitory. She'll
have to find another number on which to hang her life and happiness.
When we rely on "number satisfaction" for our emotional well-being, we
are never content.

There is a concept in psychology called *hedonic adaptation*, which
explains this continual trading-up of numbers, at least in part. *Hedonic*
means "having to do with pleasure," so the phrase refers to our mind's
ability to adjust to pleasure. Basically, the theory states that we each
have a kind of happiness thermostat or set-point. Hour to hour, day to
day our level of happiness might fluctuate slightly up and down, but we

have a general level of happiness that we settle back into.

When Joanna made her first number of $100,000, her happiness blipped for a while, but then settled back to where it usually stayed. Joanna's response, psychologically, was to decide that she had simply picked the wrong number and she traded up. The sad truth is that Joanna won't feel happy or satisfied with her life until she realizes that her expectations are holding her back—that what she needs is context and meaning, not necessarily more money.

Sneaky Numbers

Joanna chose her number based on observation of the salaries that had been achieved by others in her firm. Sara also chose her number, but her expectation of having her CD reach the "top 10" was an arbitrary choice, based mainly on the general consensus that top 10 anything in the world is excellent. But we don't always have conscious control over the numbers in our lives.

The Paradox of Numbers

As many negative examples as I've given, it's important to understand that numbers are not all negative. They are markers in our lives and they give us guidelines for when and how we can reach our potential. The problem comes when we are driven to change our negative story. Then they are exaggerated or put to the extreme.

We use numbers as targets to make up for some hurt, slight, or fragility in our personality. When that happens, they become our personal bottomless pit of frustration and dissatisfaction. But if we use numbers as a tool—instead of a goal—we can take control of our own emotions and life path.

For example, our daughter Alaina is 25. At this time in her life, numbers are everything. She has scores of them—how much she weighs, how tall she is, what kind of grades she's getting. She and her girlfriends talk about plans and markers—how old they think they will be when they get married, how much money they want to make, how many children they might have.

Many of these numbers are benchmarks that will help Alaina realize her potential. For example, there are advantages to maintaining a healthy weight. If watching your weight leads to better nutrition or a steady exercise routine, then it was a positive tool.

But if watching the scale affects your emotions, that's a sign that you might be overly-invested in that number that is your weight expectation. There are also advantages to having a salary goal in mind—it can help you negotiate your worth, buy a home and prepare for a comfortable retirement.

For any number, you need to always be questioning the truth of what you are seeking. If we take the example of money, you need to question the real value. What is it going to do for you, and what are you going to do with it? Do you have plans for it—or do you think that your life will somehow, automatically become better just because your bank account reaches a particular number?

You would be surprised at how often I hear that type of magical thinking from clients. Like the guy whose dream of attaining the corner office also included a vision of playing baseball with his son—and yet, by the time he got the office, his son was already away at college.

Then there's the woman who had the unreasonable expectation that if she could lose twenty pounds, her estranged husband would come back and love her forever...and she would get a raise at work. That would have to be a mighty powerful twenty pounds to accomplish so much.

In a way, each number is like a mother's smile—something we seek and when it arrives, we think it will light up the world. That's not truth. A mother's smile might brighten a room or your soul, but the world at large remains as it was.

If a number has nothing attached to it except your futile attempt to win love and indirectly rearrange the past, then your expectations will always, *always*, go unfulfilled. Empty, ego-driven numbers are external markers of what we should know internally.

Joanna will never be satisfied with any amount of money because she is not chasing dollars—she is reaching for a sense of meaning. She wants the validation of a number she thinks can be attained only by people with "real talent."

Sara needs the validation of *amazon.com* sales ranks. For both these individuals, the deeper issue is the doubt—the lack of faith they have in themselves. Despite their objective successes, they still aren't sure how good they are. Sara told me about a time when she heard a jazz cut on a radio station and she thought to herself, "This tune is really good." She listened to hear who it was, and as it turned out, the piece was something she had recorded fifteen years earlier. *She* was the piano player!

This revelation confused her—how could her ears deceive her into thinking she was good when she felt in her heart that she wasn't. She couldn't accept it because she didn't really believe in her own talent. She couldn't move past her PA to a new view of herself based on today's truth not yesterday's biased novel.

Putting Context to Obsession

Numbers are illusory and meaningless to happiness. Happiness does not recognize numbers. There is no such thing as "happy plus five." If we set a single number in our minds, it is common to think that if we reach it, it will lead to all other things—respect, satisfaction, self-esteem, status… the world. The expectations are not always rational.

I have told both Joanna and Sara, "You are not as great as you wish to be, but you're not as bad as you think you are." As I mentioned before, this phrase fits nearly everyone who has performance addiction (PA), even moderately. It is valuable because it provides a context to our obsession with numbers, whether they take the form of Amazon rank, quarterly bonuses, the size of one's waist, or the pounds on the scale each morning. I suspect most people who are driving toward particular numbers know they are trying to overcompensate for some slight they have endured or some set of circumstances that left them in doubt about themselves.

But knowing about our fears doesn't mean we have control over them. And on a deep level, Sara knew the origins of her number obsession, too. Sara's father was sullen and generally disapproving.

Sara realized at an early age that the only time she saw joy in her father's face was after one of her stellar athletic or musical performances. In those moments, she won approval and love, if only temporarily. It became her formula for good feelings; do something wonderful and Dad will be happy. Imagine the reward if she did something extraordinary. Imagine if she was one of the top 10 in the world. That is what led Sara to her numbers and to her unhappiness.

Both Sara and Joanna have learned—and continue to learn—that the theory they have lived by is a myth. They realize that they have been misguided in where and how they pursued love and acceptance; that they have formed an incorrect fictional story; and that their belief system is flawed. Once this is truly recognized, freedom of spirit occurs.

With liberation, we can achieve with less pressure, act with less focus on the necessity of the outcome and live without feeling trapped by expectations.

Expectations lift our spirits and excite us neurochemically. They can also, however, depress our spirits and elicit negative neurochemicals if, rather than being based on actualizing potential they are efforts to overcome wounds of childhood. We must understand that expectations fuel our spirit, but the attained goal will lose its significance over time, especially if we have hidden reasons for our pursuits.

When Sara told me she hated music, I knew she was having a visceral reaction to her over-inflated expectations. She didn't hate music. She hated the obsessive nature that she had imposed on music.

I asked her if she played or sang when she was alone at home. She said yes, that the only time she loved playing and singing was when she was alone. Well, there was her answer. Because she placed so much importance, emphasis and pressure on the number, she stopped enjoying her natural gifts. The numbers took away from her intrinsic enjoyment.

The key for Sara was to peel back the layers of expectation, to experience again the natural joy, natural interest, and natural inherent capability and encourage it to flourish.

Instead of taking every gig, I encouraged Sara to play what she likes.

She started turning down concerts that pay well, but would have had her playing more commercial music she didn't like as much. Instead of large venues, she plays in small, intimate jazz houses. The last time I saw Sara, she had just sung the night before to a packed house in Boston. She was looser, more carefree and her body seemed more fluid.

"I kind of lost myself in the music," Sara said. "I was singing real jazz."

"At any point in the night, did you think about how many CDs you sold?" I asked.

She thought for a moment before smiling. "No. It was just fun." It was the beginning of her freeing herself from her misguided thinking.

Questions to Journal:

Again, I encourage you to journal your answers to the following questions, and then take steps to get grounded in experience.

- Do you identify with Sara or Joanna's story?

- Did you find yourself having any particular emotional reaction to either of their struggles?

- Are you intrinsically or extrinsically motivated? Explain.

- How did you learn either orientation?

- From whom did you learn your motivational orientation?

- What are the significant numbers in your life? Explain.

- Do you consistently calculate how much money you are making on a daily basis? If so "Why?"

- Are you particularly affected by the number associated with your chronological age?

- What are the myths you have come to realize regarding the expectations that have led you astray?

- What are realistic expectations for you to set in the future that would allow for healthy living and high accomplishment?

- Do you think it's possible to have realistic expectations, accomplish at high levels and lead a healthy life?

- What stands in your way regarding this possibility?

- Do you share with others your hopes and dreams in terms of what you imagine will make you happy?

- Have your predictions as far as what would make you feel full filled been accurate in the past?

- What have you learned from your style of setting expectations that has not worked in your best inter-est?

Get Grounded In Experience:

1. Record in your journal exactly what you expect will make you happy in the next week. Examine and record the accuracy of your predictions at weeks end.

2. Share your expectations of what will bring you joy with others, and ask them if they agree that these occurrences will make you happy based on how they have come to know you.

Chapter 4:
Liberate Yourself from the Past—Regrets and Unfulfilled Dreams

Many of us are capable of making different life choices, but we become emotionally paralyzed and helpless (that is, we don't think we can live and choose freely) because we feel emotionally imprisoned. Our unresolved novel, as we will see in the following story, can keep us believing there is no way of moving past our imperfections.

This chapter explores the nature of regret and unfulfilled dreams and how they can disrupt the positive course of our lives. Lifting these weights can be a powerful experience, allowing us to move freely into the future with energy and courage. To help illustrate these concepts, I focus on the story of Frank.

Frank came to me as a result of his wife telling him he needed to do something about his anger or she would file for divorce. He was prone to temper tantrums and easily frustrated when things in his business and family life did not go well. He turned to drinking to "take the edge off" and eventually needed more and more alcohol to do the job.

Frank loved his children dearly but was unusually hard on his twin sons; only his youngest daughter escaped his wrath by adopting his extreme work ethic and athletic excellence. Frank came to me a beaten man, ashamed of his behavior, yet feeling powerless to control his anger, his frustration and his tremendous guilt for the past. In fact, I had seldom met anyone with the level of pervasive guilt Frank experienced. He clearly wanted to be punished!

"You can put me in my place; tell me I'm an idiot. I'm here to get better and I'll do anything to save my family." Frank was literally begging me to help, pleading for the way to overcome his past.

Apologies only matter if they are accompanied by changed behavior. Frank's shame kept him from talking to his adult children and from facing his wife with a request for forgiveness. Instead, he showered them with fancy vacations, tickets to key sporting events, etc.

I never met a human being who managed his time so efficiently; his business ran like a smooth boat gliding across the water. He worked 15 hour days, 6 days a week and on Sunday he worked on his home tirelessly.

His demands for excellence in those around him were unrelenting and he seldom took the time to thank others for their efforts, thinking praise would lead others to take advantage of him. This behavior caused others to lose focus and work less effectively.

Frank is an extremely intense man; he seldom feels calm and consequently, my office soon became a place of refuge for him. I could see as weeks passed that his guilt was lessening, not dramatically, but it was lessening. How did this occur?

Guilt and Grandiosity are First Cousins

Frank's level of guilt equaled his imagined level of importance. "I am a go-to guy. I get things done, and everyone knows that about me. If you want a ticket to a Red Sox game, I'm your man. You need a favor with a banker, I can make the contact. My family knows I can solve any crisis, but it wears me out."

I am not minimizing Frank's guilt, as it shows he has a conscience and it demonstrates concern for others, but often those with excessive guilt are imagining that without their input or presence, people would be drastically affected.

I once told Frank, "Someday we will both die and despite what you think, our families will survive without us. People remarry, children become adults and many people who have lost a father, husband and boss are still functioning in the world today."

He found this new perspective humbling at first, but eventually it lifted a burden for him. He had used his guilt to accentuate his importance. He initially felt a loss of esteem with this new perspective, but he realized over time that it was the truth.

I asked him to miss one of his son's high school soccer games as an experiment. He had never missed a game in three years. Guess what? Allen didn't even ask his dad where he was; I suspect he felt relieved to not have to worry about his dad's critique after the game.

In time, Frank came to realize he had guilt for his misdeeds, but he also maintained a level of guilt to support his imagined worth with people.

Some People Get Their Loving from Fighting

Frank and his wife Elaine have been in a contentious marriage for years. They fight, make up and fight again. They call each other unflattering names, critique each other's actions and blame each other for the lack of connection they feel. They are like two boxers in a ring, constantly jabbing at each other yet remaining attached throughout the contest.

Their sexual relationship has always been intense; it is the one way they feel love for each other. Expressing positive feelings toward each other seldom occurs, although they both long to hear a sentence of two that will give them a special feeling.

When they have differences of opinion, they go into "cold war" mode, both refusing to speak about anything relevant, resulting in the penalty they both pay for their refusal to address conflict directly.

Frank is not comfortable with intimacy, plain and simple. He grew up in a family where arguing was the norm, both parents competing for control. His mother often won and his father would de-invest into a bottle of scotch. Frank learned the same method.

His father owned a car dealership. Frank owns several today and his business success never suffered, despite the consequences suffered by his family. Frank worked for his father for five years after high school. They argued frequently over business strategy and eventually Frank's fury took over and his father threw him off the car lot.

Frank stopped speaking to both parents and during that time his mother had a fatal heart attack. His two brothers, his father and most of his relatives blamed him for her death. He attended the funeral and his father told his brothers to "Get him the hell out of here," while yelling at Frank, "Are you proud? See what you did to her?"

The accumulated guilt from his mother's death propelled Frank into heavy drinking, late hours at bars, while developing in him decreasingly less tolerance for even the slightest conflict with people. Emotional hypersensitivity is a common symptom of alcoholism and even for those in early recovery.

It was during this time that his wife became more aggressive with him. Her approach did not help the situation as her combative style furthered his guilt, and her criticisms were not mild, "You ruined one family, now you're doing the same to ours."

He started his own business, struggled the first few years, but eventually became a success. Of course this all occurred at great expense to his health and his family. When I met him he was overweight, drinking heavily, hadn't exercised in years and looked well beyond his 42 years.

Change is an Active Process

As the weeks went by, Frank began to feel more comfortable with me. He was quite honest and would follow my guidance as best he could. He started attending AA meetings, obtained a sponsor, and was sober for four months on his first try. He relapsed after an argument with one of his sons but eventually used his contacts in AA to regain his focus. As of today he has been sober for three years.

At one point I recommended that he join one of my group-coaching sessions and he immediately said no. "Doc, I can talk to you. I mean, I know you're not judging me, but I could never tell strangers about myself this way. I haven't even told my friends in AA about all this stuff."

We continued to talk about his difficulty managing conflict with people and his reluctance to be direct with his children, wife and employees. He conceded that these were interpersonal problems, the kind I described he could work on in group sessions. He decided to give it a try, as he needed to improve steadily to restore his life.

In group meetings Frank learned to be more empathic toward others. He struggled for some time, learning to be tactfully direct rather than aggressive. This was difficult for him because he usually stored up feelings and when he expressed directly it was with anger and without anyone's feelings in mind.

Once irritation had built up and he felt "right" about an issue, he would eventually blow up. I could read his face often in group discussions. It was not difficult to see when he was bothered by someone's point of view or when he was affected by a certain individual. I would ask him at those times what he was experiencing. He would hesitate, but with some coaching he would express himself, always thinking he was going to engender a negative response. He grew up in an environment where direct communication tended to mean a fight. The idea of conflict resolution was actually a foreign experience for him.

Frank learned over time that he was quite insightful as group members really valued his feedback. He also learned to take in some of the negative comments without reacting defensively.

I remember one morning when a female member told him he was too intense, that he scared her and she could understand why his wife started to fight back. Rather than reacting impulsively, he began to tear, "I thought I had made progress but I guess I have a lot of work to do."

He was sharing vulnerability rather than throwing a punch, a significant change indeed. Slowly but surely, Frank settled into the group process. He was changing and he felt this movement internally in a powerful way.

Now the work was to take his new interpersonal skills, his new knowledge of what he had been recreating from the past and apply these new insights to the present. He had the awareness to rewrite his novel, but this could only happen by his addressing the most important people in his life.

He had to have conversations with his children and his wife. It did not go well at first, but they are still moving forward every week. His wife has trouble forgiving him, but she is trying. His children are most appreciative of his newfound skills. They respect his courage and dedication to change.

Frank has become what I call a *Spiritual Learner*; someone who, throughout his life, seeks the truth about himself, his true nature and seeks to understand the truth of others as well.

Spiritual Learners are intimately involved in the world, relate to a diverse group of people and seek meaning and knowledge from all credible sources. They are committed to taking care of their body, soul and all others they can help in a positive manner. We will talk more about *Spiritual Learners* throughout this book. It is a way of being that I believe is vital to our lifestyle, our health and our overall success.

Today, Frank sponsors young men from diverse backgrounds in the AA program. He relates to those of different faiths with appreciation rather than how he has in the past, and without a sense of threat.

He is involved with several groups in his local community and his view of people has expanded considerably. "I learned in the group from everyone, people I probably would have never thought I had much in common with. Truth is, we are all seeking the same thing—peace of mind and spirit."

Frank, as all my group members, has initiated an exercise program. I try to include the latest science related to overall health in our sessions, and there is no doubt that exercise changes brain chemistry and is the best anti-depressant God ever created.

Frank has taken this information seriously and has been walking and doing strength training for over a year now. He now looks younger than his age and has an attitude of engagement when meeting people rather than his previous reticence.

A new member recently joined our group and after her first session thanked Frank for being so understanding and assuring. These are abilities his wife is beginning to appreciate.

Frank is still learning every week; his efforts are genuine and consistent. He is on the path to becoming the man he always wanted to be.

Change is an active process and regrets can only be overcome with new behavior. Genuine understanding of one's previous behavior and the effect we have had on others is crucial to progress.

Frank is less regretful because he has had direct conversations with his wife and adult children. He has asked them how he has affected them, sat silently and listened rather than defending himself as he used to do.

They are forgiving him because they see he is genuinely sorry and responds differently today. He is more patient, tolerant and much less perfectionistic. He has many friendships in the AA program and has decided to go back to college to become an addiction counselor; he is a prime example of how we tend to teach our own struggles.

Frank's dream was to be an extremely successful CEO and to be a great husband and father. He attained the first, but in order to attain his unfulfilled dream, he had to establish a new kind of relationship with his family. He had to apologize, but more than acknowledging his mistakes, he had to develop interpersonal abilities to change the present.

He began relating in a way that truly increased love rather than causing the uneasiness of the past. One of his twin sons, now a college sophomore, recently said, "I have never felt comfortable being with my dad until today."

If you suffer from regret or unfulfilled dreams, you may feel worthless, ineffective and unsuccessful. You probably have difficulty making decisions and may be prone to changing your mind. When you overcome this second challenge so that you are no longer fixated on toxic wishes, you gain confidence and become free to move into the future with energy and courage.

What's Your Wish? Choose Wisely

When Aladdin found the genie in the magic lamp, he was granted three wishes. Thanks to Disney's animated movie, children everywhere dream of what joy they could find if they were allowed even a single wish.

What about you—what would you wish?

In the abstract, the most common wish is for more money, because most people believe that money will buy happiness and freedom. But if you really dig deep, the true wishes arise.

I see clients every week who wish they had never had an affair, or that they had more children, finished college, or that they pursued a different career. In other words, they have regrets.

Regret is a destructive wish, a desire to undo some action that causes us sadness or shame. By focusing on what might have been, we remove ourselves from living fully in the present. Regret is a terrible weight to bear. I see it as a huge boulder that sits smack in the middle of our psyches. Every now and then, we roll it over and allow it to crush any joy we might be feeling. Don't get me wrong—I'm not blaming anyone for making bad decisions. We all have regrets.

My younger brother took his own life several years ago and for years I was devastated with regret for things I might have done to help him through that tragic time. It took me years to talk about the end of his life. Eventually, I spoke more and more as it was having a devastating effect on my outlook on the present and the future. Those closest to me have told me numerous times that it wasn't my fault and I appreciate their intentions, but I know I could have done better.

Since his death, I have helped many people in exactly the same circumstance. My only consolation is trying to understand that the knowledge and understanding I have today, I did not have then. Learning from the experience and adopting new behavior is the only way I have found to lessen the regret and move forward.

In the end, what other choice do we have? We can hold onto depression, wish and hope to redo the past, but we can't. On the other hand, we are responsible for changing and learning today. There is a saying in AA, "You're not responsible for your disease but you are responsible for your recovery."

Some people, however, seem to hold on to their regret. A few seem almost proud of it, as though their self-professed failures are what define them as human beings. Others deny their regrets and end up subconsciously rehashing the remnants of shame with which they never came to terms.

It is a tragic irony that as we get older and have more life experiences behind us (and therefore more opportunities to take a mistaken turn,) we have a greater appreciation for what we want in life and a greater risk of regret.

I have treated many men who have worked obsessively throughout their lives, building reputations, careers, and retirement funds only to experience profound regret once they reach age 50 or 60.

Once their children are young adults, out of college, and perhaps married with families of their own, these high-powered men regret the time they spent away from their growing children and the lost closeness with their wives.

Once they retire, the connection to their only significant social network at work is severed. They discover that they are shut out from the sweet and tender part of family life and all their earnings can't buy them a place in their children's memories.

If they are self-aware and lucky, these men find comfort in their grandchildren. They become super grandparents, overcompensating for neglecting the previous generation. They find their freedom late, but not too late.

Another type of destructive wish is the unrealistic dream, a desire that could never have come true regardless of action. While regret describes a wish that *might* have been, unrealistic dreams describes wishes that *never* could have been because they are contrary to reality.

One sad example is my client Ruth, a 50-year-old woman whose dream is to walk into a room and be the most beautiful woman present. She desperately wanted to be, in her words, "drop-dead gorgeous," envied by women, desired by men and able to command attention with nothing more than the force of her beauty.

In reality, Ruth is an attractive-looking woman. Attractive, however, is not enough for Ruth. She has longed to be drop-dead gorgeous since she was a little girl. This particular dream was carved into her heart in childhood. As a chubby girl, Ruth endured the teasing of her father and brothers who never let her forget that she was not very pretty. It's hard to get over the nickname "Fattycakes."

Over the years, after spending tens of thousands of dollars on designer clothes, age crept up and threatened to shred what little self-esteem Ruth had. That's when her beauty quest turned dangerous. She has been able to maintain normal weight by exercising—not 30 minutes, not an hour, but a *minimum* of three hours a day.

Recently, Ruth learned that this obsessive level of activity has contributed to the development of osteoporosis. When her doctor told her she would have to scale back the exercise or risk serious bone loss, she opted to keep exercising, preferring fractures to weight gain.

At this low point in her life, instead of letting go of the unrealistic dream, she went one step further and got cosmetic surgery—a face lift and breast implants. It turned into a nightmare. The implants became infected and needed to be removed, but they had been in place too long. The skin stretched, leaving sunken craters in her chest.

Today, Ruth cannot stand to look at herself in a mirror and everyone who knows her believes that she has squandered her life pursuing a dream that never could have come true. This wish has given her nothing but heartache, illness and disfigurement. It didn't have to be this way.

You don't need to be gorgeous to free yourself from the negative hardwiring of childhood.

I wish I could say that Ruth has resolved her unrealistic dream, but it has not happened yet. Yes, she can control her focus on her body somewhat; she can move away from thoughts of "being ugly, being fat" and concentrate on other aspects of her personality with some success.

I think the greatest relief for her is to hear from other group members, male and female, that they all worry about appearance. We are in a culture that floods us with images of perfect bodies; none of us escapes this conditioning entirely.

She has also found relief from the comments of the male members in particular. Early on George commented to her that he wished she would let herself be known. She argued, "But I tell you all of my anxieties every week, my hatred of my body, my face."

"Yes," he replied, "but all you're sharing is your obsession, nothing at all about other aspects of who you are, and what you're involved with in life."

Ruth realized, over time, how unappealing this tendency had become and how very narrow her own view of herself had become. These new men in her life were not her brothers; they were genuinely interested in her as a human being.

This work helped her to become aware of when she was obsessing out loud and it made a considerable difference in all her relationships. Her girlfriends have noticed and are enjoying her more and her boyfriend told her he finally feels she has let him in, not just "in" on her anxieties but "in" on her intimate feelings about life.

She is becoming a well-rounded person rather than an individual with a faulty belief system. Her dream to be Angelina Jolie, adored by the Brad Pitts of the world, is slowly being replaced by real intimacy, real love and real friendship with real people.

Ruth had a dream to "be somebody," to rewrite her novel and become the desired one rather than the ordinary girl her brothers mocked.

Often we are unaware that our dreams are not motivated by our inherent desires but are driven by an attempt to finally, once and for all, measure up, be good enough, belong and be accepted.

Last summer one of my clients was planning on attending his high school reunion. He really wanted to show people how successful he had become so he planned to rent a Porsche for a day. As the evening progressed he became increasingly disappointed; nobody seemed to notice his image car.

As the night went on, he retreated to the bar where he met an old friend, another guy who felt he was not the star he was in high school. After several drinks his classmate confessed to him that he had rented a BMW sports car for the event. They both ended up having a great night, laughing about how silly they were acting at age 38. They continued to stay connected, have introduced each other to their wives and children and this summer the two families will vacation together. Rob didn't wow anyone with the Porsche, but he found a friend that ultimately meant more than impressing fellow classmates, people he will only see every five to ten years.

Questions to Journal:

- With what aspects of Frank's story did you relate?

- Did you have any particular emotional reaction to his plight?

- Did you identify with any aspect of Ruth's story? Explain.

- What were your emotional reactions to these stories?

- How about Rob's futile attempt to achieve status—what are your reactions?

- How prevalent is guilt in your life?

- How much does guilt govern your behavior and your thinking?

- Do you see the correlation between chronic guilt and grandiosity?

- Can you describe how that dynamic might function inside you?

- When you apologize for your behavior, is it accompanied with behavioral change?

- If not, why do you express regret without changing your errant behavior?

- Have you wished you could undo the past in any particular way?

- What do you want to reverse in your life story?

- What difference do you think it would make in your life?

- Have you had the courage to ask others close to you if they agree?

- Do you have unrealistic dreams that you think will make up for your unsupportive story?

- What do you find yourself wishing for in terms of changing the past?

- Frank, Ruth and Rob wanted desperately to rewrite their stories to alter their fragile sense of self. Do you have the same quest? Explain.

- How can you accomplish your wish in a constructive way?

- What do you think allows a person to actually let go of past regrets and unfulfilled dreams and live fully in the present?

Get Grounded in Experience:

1. What is your most recent regret? What dream have you failed to realize in the last year? Find out from those close to you whether they consider your regret and dream realistic, or based on a faulty story containing performance addiction. Is it really hurting their view of you?

Chapter 5:
Loosen the Reins and Lift the Burden— Control

No matter how strong, wealthy or authoritative a person is control eventually fails. Whether loss of control is permanent or short term is often influenced by our particular ability to cope.

When we are faced with unforeseen circumstances, we must learn how to deal with the change and to adjust to a life in which our elemental belief in control is shattered. I have clients who have dealt with this challenge in the form of parapalegia, the death of a child, development of a disabling autoimmune disease and unexpected divorce.

Some individuals experience loss of control as a threat to their sense of self, leaving them confused. Some individuals blame God, especially when causality is a mystery—such as childhood cancers or fatal car accidents—and they feel singled out for punishment from a vengeful universe. Those who overcome the third challenge learn to live with their fate without obsessing over what used to be, and without losing their sense of self. Instead, they develop a new life within those new circumstances.

In this chapter, I discuss three clients—one who has regained control over his life after becoming paralyzed in a fall, one who is overcoming the dreadful scare of breast cancer, and one who had become emotionally paralyzed and unable to deal with the loss of control she experienced when she became intimate with the wrong man.

I also relate a very personal story of how I watched my own mother lose all control of her life and ultimately regain a stronger sense of herself through the loss of her youngest son. The goal of telling these stories is to help you understand that salvation is always possible—success is relative to the given situation.

If you suffer from control issues, you may feel as though you are constantly doing battle with others—they don't listen, they misbehave, they don't respect your opinions or authority. You may feel that your actions don't or can't change anything.

There are two possible responses: if you are in active engagement, you probably feel angry or frustrated much of the time; or if you have given up, you may feel depressed and fatigued. When you overcome this third challenge, you gain mental flexibility, stamina and peace of mind.

A Courageous Heart

Paul fell off a roof and became paralyzed. He owned his own roofing business, so he was used to scaling buildings, walking great heights and using potentially fatal power tools. On this day, he was in a hurry to make a dentist appointment. His attention dropped, his foot slipped and the next thing he knew he was on his back struggling to breathe.

Most people understand that life is, almost by definition, uncontrollable. If we eat well, exercise, avoid smoking and generally take good care of ourselves, we are likely to remain healthier and live longer than people who have less meticulous personal habits; but not always. Bad things happen even to those who do everything right. Non-smokers can get lung cancer; former valedictorians can lose their jobs in a downsizing; active, 35-year-old men can slip off a roof.

Eventually, control fails us all, often in ways that we can't even imagine. Our bodies change, our families change or people move away or die. But nature's cruel joke is that, as we age, many people lose the flexibility and energy they need to deal with change.

People who remain open to new experiences and who expand their social circle have an expanded capacity for learning. Their brains develop new neurons. They find life interesting, not a chore. They like to find the novelty in every situation and "mix it up" a little, as opposed to the routine predictability I often see in many of my adult clients.

When your life changes, will you dust yourself off and spread your wings again? Will you be able to adjust to a new life if your elemental belief in control is shattered? Will you be a *spiritual learner* or retreat into a position of regret; or worse, fall into a state of helplessness?

Paul lives near the church where I rent space to do my group sessions. After group on Friday mornings, I meet Paul at his home for our weekly session.

One Friday morning I was early and arrived before him. I talked with Ronnie, a recovering drug addict who is staying with Paul—not because Paul needs help, but because Ronnie needs to put his life back together. Ronnie lost his job, his wife, his driver's license and most of his friends because of cocaine; and he is having trouble figuring out how to adapt to the circumstances of his life.

When Paul arrived, he roared up on the motorcycle he had custom-outfitted for his particular disability. He had come from the lake where he was overseeing the construction of a dock at a camp for handicapped children so they could learn how to kayak and water ski. Last winter, Paul went skiing on a special ski with his young son in Aspen. He also won a deep sea fishing contest with his son in Canada this past summer.

None of these achievements came easily. In fact, Paul went through a profound depression after the accident. Paul's wife eventually filed for divorce, continuing a time in his life that seemed like the worst nightmare possible.

I lived through Paul's depression. I visited him in a Boston hospital after I learned he was paralyzed. His first words to me were, "Doc, can you believe this happened to me? What am I going to do? I could lose my business. How will I support my family? This is crazy. I can't live like this! You know I can't!" I cried when I left his room. I felt empty with a deep sense of sadness as I drove home, wondering how I could help Paul and how he could ultimately help himself.

How could this man, in his late 30's, very successful, two homes, real estate, land purchases, see it all come crumbling down and recover? His wife had left him. Two years later his father developed leukemia; then his mother discovered she had breast cancer. The only friend he felt understood his plight was a fellow paraplegic he met in rehab. Unfortunately, his friend committed suicide shortly thereafter, not being able to cope with the life of a paraplegic. We started our journey with a momentous mountain in our path.

The first two years of our meetings were filled with grief, anger and despair. I listened as Paul told me how much he missed walking, running and skating. He'd been a stellar athlete and a very physical man all his life. How could he ever work out again? How could he regain his business? Would he disappoint his son? He was afraid he wouldn't be able to teach him how to hit a baseball, fish, ski, etc. Would his ex-wife's new boyfriend take his place in his son's heart?

All these fears filled his mind, all based on a loss of complete control. I had seen this kind of despair before; the look in a person's eyes when they feel all control over their life is lost. When my brother David died I was the one to tell my mother. As I entered our family home, I didn't speak a word. My mother hugged my brother's high school picture and started sobbing, "He's gone, I know he's gone." She had great intuition and had known instantly. She had worried about him constantly and her worst nightmare had come true.

My father always seemed to be the stronger of my parents. A hero of the Second World War, he was known for facing each crisis with courage. However, he fell apart in the face of losing his son. He seemed almost dazed at times, muttering to himself in the funeral home, focusing on inconsequential things, staring into space and seeming like he was somewhere else.

My mother, I feared, was losing control completely. Weeping, crying out in pain. At the cemetery she walked toward to the casket as I held her hand, then suddenly she fell onto the casket. I pulled her up, fearing she was about to fall in with my brother. I realized at that moment that it was what she wanted. My mother was not a dramatic woman; she just could not bear the loss. Her heart was shattered and she wanted to join him.

I was teaching at a college in Connecticut at the time, about to begin writing my doctoral dissertation. I would call my parents often, if not daily, after the funeral. I could not tolerate the sadness in their voices. My mother seemed to worry about me more every week, taking an unusually cautious stance; she obviously could not bear to lose another son. I couldn't write any longer and was too preoccupied with the loss of my brother and my parents' depression, so I decided to leave my position and return home to be with them and hopefully finish my degree.

Something unusual happened upon my return. I had anticipated it would be unbearably depressing to live with my parents again, especially in lieu of what had happened. It was just the opposite. I had the best discussions I had ever had with my mother.

At the time I was very interested in reading and learning about the major religions. I was raised Roman Catholic but was ever curious about other points of view. I read about Judaism, Tibetan Buddhism, Hinduism, Taoism and the various Protestant sects. I was amazed one morning to see my mother reading one of my Buddhist texts. She was curious, wanting to learn more and discuss its contents. She was searching and I was encouraged that she was open to all possibilities.

I was studying the martial arts at the time and I would see her in the backyard practicing some of the stretching routines I would do in the morning. Eventually, she began studying yoga and, as I wrote my dissertation, she would type each page, always asking me questions about one theory of human behavior versus another.

Of course she would also ask the questions I dreaded: "Why do young people take their own lives? Is it their parent's fault? Is it our society? What could possibly drive someone to feel such despair?"

My mother became a *spiritual learner*; her broken heart had propelled her toward learning all she could to understand as much as she could. This woman, who'd left the seventh grade to go to work, never seeing the insides of a high school classroom, had not only acquired a wealth of wisdom, but her manner of learning was open. She was free to integrate knowledge. She was not wedded to one point of view, one religion, or one psychology theory.

I never answered her questions definitively. We both accepted at one point that there wasn't one answer but many. The more she learned, the less preoccupied she seemed with "the answer" and more acceptant of the many variables that drive our behavior. She became less needy of certainty, less focused on absolutes and more at ease with the realities of life.

My love for my mother deepened during those days. I had always loved her a great deal but never appreciated her courage. She amazed me! I expected her to withdraw into a position of helplessness as she lost control, but instead she gained more authority over her life than ever before.

Loss of control often leads to gaining control. My mother died at age 59 of breast cancer, a few years after my brother. My father commented at her funeral that it was like being at the "league of nations." People from all races, religions and walks of life attended. It was truly the greatest compliment to her.

Interestingly, I saw this same process take place in Paul's life—constantly asking me what I thought about regaining his business, how to continue his role as a father and whether he would ever drive again. We found a physical therapist who would train him to condition his upper body so that he could move more adeptly in his chair. He called truck manufacturers to see if a vehicle could be made for him to drive. We talked about how he could train men to be part of his roofing business. He eventually trained two men, and he even had them hoist him up on to the very roof he'd fallen from to face his fear and most importantly, "to finish that goddamn job."

We made a plan to call old customers to let them know he was back in business. He asked the baseball commissioner of his son's league if he could coach his team. Last spring they won their division and his son could not be more proud of his dad.

Today, Paul's business is thriving. He goes to job sites daily and works out at a gym three times a week. He has made his home handicap accessible and has become a great cook. He had abandoned his church after the accident, but today he and his son attend every Sunday morning. "It gives me such a good feeling to be there with Jr."

Paul's Takeaway

A few weeks ago, after one of our individual sessions, Paul remarked, "I am a better person as a paraplegic."

The tragedies of Paul's accident made him slow down and reflect as the circumstances overwhelmed him with emotion. He was not known for expressing feelings readily. Loss of control can be a blessing. It can actually lift a burden one has been carrying all through life.

Paul tried so very hard to control all aspects of his life—his work environment, his wife, his son, etc. He always thought he was doing the "right thing." He never realized that people could not relax around him. They worried he would be easily displeased or that they would disappoint him if they didn't make that "all-out" effort he encouraged.

Today he has learned how to listen rather than using his old style of lecturing. He can tolerate vulnerability rather than giving anyone who has a doubt a pep talk. He understands human frailty in a way he never considered before. As a result, people feel closer to him and he feels closeness with many people he never experienced closeness with before.

Deep Within

I have been through the same experience with others who have lost control, whether permanent or temporary. Clients who have had breast cancer, prostate cancer, lost a child due to an accident—all had that same look in their eyes. "How can I possibly cope when everything is out of my control?"

And then, as emotions are discussed and thoughts are aired over and over again, something begins to change (particularly if they are letting their deepest experiences become known to a person or persons who are mirroring back interest, concern, honesty and especially empathy.) At least for some this is true; total despair is transformed into a courageous outlook on life. We could call this perspective a spiritual outlook.

Some individuals, to their own surprise, rise out of despair to become *spiritual learners*. Something happens to them that make them want to learn all they can from any credible source. They most likely have had this resilience somewhere within and were probably never called on to deal with life's harshest realities until their current situation.

One of my clients I saw today had both breasts and lymph nodes removed three months ago. At the time, Nicole told me she didn't think she could cope with chemotherapy and God forbid radiation.

Today she has completed her fourth round of chemo, lost her hair and nevertheless I saw in her eyes an expression of hope. "I hate this; some days I cry the whole day. But unlike before, I think I will make it. I know one thing: when this is over, I am going to want more out of life and more out of myself. I want to be everything I can be. No more holding things in, trying to please everyone at my own expense. I want more from life—more passion, more intimacy and more knowledge."

I hadn't seen Nicole since she had her operation, although we had talked briefly on the phone. At the end of every night, I pray on my knees. I always include Nicole in my prayers. I pray for her to have courage, to emerge with vitality and health from this experience. I pray she would live a long life free of illness.

I am sure many others have prayed for her as well; she is the kind of person who is easy to like. My prayers were answered when I saw determination in her face. Regardless of the outcome, she has become a person who is destined to live life to the fullest.

Paul, Nicole and my mother are the type of people that lift our spirits because they cope with the loss of control in the most constructive ways possible. They dig deep and rise above the situation, defy odds and somehow emerge with more integrity and wisdom than they ever had before.

These outcomes are not accidental; to triumph in these situations demands a belief in oneself that is embedded at the deepest level of our existence. Somewhere through the years of their lives, these individuals looked into the mirror of another extremely influential human being and the reflection said, "You're a very special person with amazing abilities."

For many people, this experience of positive mirroring did not take place in childhood but occurred later in life, either through friendships, love relationships such as marriage, a parenting experience and possibly through work colleagues. For many people this experience takes place through involvement in psychotherapy, especially in a group coaching experience. However it happened, somewhere along the way, these individuals internalized the faith others had in them and made it their own.

No Control over Love

Unfortunately, not everyone follows such a positive course, even when the opportunities are presented to them. Sometimes childhood trauma has been too great to entirely reverse. I am a believer that these kinds of changes can occur when people engage in the process of transformation with conviction and dedication. Some people, however, hold on to their untrue novel despite mounds of evidence to the contrary.

How is it that so many people, when they lose control temporarily, make it a permanent state of mind?

My client, Rebecca, is a good example. She is an immigrant from Greece who came to the United States at age eight. Her parents' marriage was always problematic; her father drank heavily most nights. He seldom reacted to his children except when they were irritating him by being children. Her mother acquiesced to her husband, making sure his temper was not set off. She took care of all domestic and parental duties.

Rebecca's father was physical with her and her brother. Her mother watched silently, seldom offering protection. In confidence she would encourage her daughter to never marry, saying, "Men are all the same; they only want one thing."

Rebecca skipped school most of sixth grade and her parents never noticed. She was eventually discovered by a school official in late March of the same school year. Her father slapped her once, neither parent asking any relevant questions as to "why" she was truant and life went on.

She was molested by a neighbor the year after but never told her parents, thinking it would be useless. "They would just blame me or not believe me." As a result she developed an angry attitude toward the world, believing that nobody cared and people were basically "out to get anything they can from you."

She had few friends in high school and dropped out of a community college when she felt rejected by her first boyfriend. He cheated on her frequently and eventually left her for another girl she knew well, someone "much skinnier and prettier than me."

Subsequently she drank heavily on weekends and developed bulimia to manage her difficulty with her weight. When I met her at age 25, she had already seen four psychiatrists over a period of five years and had been on several anti-depressants, which reportedly had little effect on her low mood.

She had been hospitalized for psychiatric reasons twice, made three suicide attempts and would cut herself to release pain (the cutting releases opiates that dull the pain of loss and rejection.) Rebecca became quite addicted to this pattern of release.

Upon our first meeting, she related in a very passive-aggressive style, saying little and implying that any efforts to understand her had already been tried. She made sure I knew she could kill herself at any time and was quite proud to show me where she cut herself on her arm.

Rebecca's self esteem was clearly elevated when she could defeat an authority figure. She described the last psychiatrist she saw as a "pill pusher" who looked like he needed therapy himself. She commented on his poor dress habits, how he was overweight and she criticized him for taking notes as she talked. I learned quickly that Rebecca had few kind words to say about anyone, always highlighting how people have disappointed her in one way or another.

We met for some time in individual sessions. Then I took a big gamble and added her to one of my group coaching sessions. I knew that Rebecca's belief that she was unlovable and unworthy was so strong, that only the power of a group experience could possibly alter her thinking and the way she perceived others.

Today Rebecca has a respected job in a corporation, exercises daily, is off all medication and is not usually depressed. She has given up bulimic behavior and is respected by members of the group (although not always liked.) She remains single and has unfortunately given up on the possibility of ever being in a relationship. She still struggles with viewing relationships as a battle for control. "There are no equal relationships; someone always has the control, the upper hand. I don't trust myself. I would let someone take over again and I would lose all the gains I've made."

Rebecca, at least to this point, can't believe (or is afraid to believe) that equality can exist in an intimate relationship. I don't know anyone who longs for love more than Rebecca. Sadly, her fear of losing control is as great as her longing for love.

Rebecca can be quite insightful and has been recognized in the group as one of the most honest, direct members. However, she had to learn how to speak the truth without attempting to humiliate the other person. She joined a sophisticated group of people. When she would go on the attack, someone would inevitably label her insecurity and comment on how threatened she seemed.

One man, whose opinion she valued highly, told her one night that he admired her insight and her ability to read people but that she communicated "like a sniper" enjoying the kill.

These interactions hurt her and she would become defensive. Ultimately however, she came to see that people were giving her feedback to help, not hurt her. As a result, she developed the first trusting relationships in her life.

She obviously has made many gains. Her anger has dissipated, her ability to get along with others has improved dramatically, her ability to take care of her body has improved and her ability to manage conflict assertively rather than aggressively has also improved.

However, her fear of loss of control if she becomes intimate with a man is still pervasive and may always be so. She is at a juncture in her life: hold on to the gains made and be moderately happy or take a risk to grow further and risk the possibility of being hurt again. Of course, she could also achieve the richness of intimate love that she has never known.

Slavery to Our Minds

It is amazing to me, that as control of one's own life is compromised by life circumstances, a creative spirit can arise to create a solution, an outcome with the possibility of freedom—freedom from the nightmare of emotional oppression and most importantly freedom from the fictionalized view of oneself that has been so embedded.

People often ask me how I can be optimistic when dealing with the tragedies in people's lives. It is the Paul's of the world that make any adversity seem resolvable. I know it may sound naïve, but I do believe it is far healthier to be on this side of the coin than embracing the perspective that Rebecca holds onto so tightly.

I continue to work with Rebecca because I think there is that possibility that she may rewrite her complete story someday. She may heal her wounds and free her heart to fall into the arms of an honest, loving, ethical man. Control lost often equals love gained.

Questions to Journal:

- With what aspect of Paul's story do you relate?

- How do you imagine you would cope with the loss of control he suffered?

- Could you imagine coping as well as he has over time?

- How have you reacted to the concept of the spiritual learner?

- Do you need an inordinate amount of control in your life?

- If so, what function does being preoccupied with being in control have for your sense of self or your self-worth?

- What have you learned about the purpose of your holding on to control when it is impractical?

- Do you have any of the fears Rebecca experiences when she contemplates losing control?

- What past hurts have caused you to hold on tightly to control?

- How will you change your life story so you can let go of the excessive need for control?

- How does your need for control relate to performance addiction?

- How does your need for control relate to perfectionism?

- How does your need for control interfere with your intimate relationships?

- How does your need for control protect you from your lack of trust in other people?

- Do you ever trust anyone enough to just "let go?"

- What would it be like for you to give up control and expose your vulnerabilities to a group of people?

- Is it too threatening to imagine? Why?

Get Grounded In Experience:

1. In the immediate future, what aspect of losing control might affect you the most? Let your mind wander and try to answer spontaneously.

2. Plan to confront this fear while expressing your emotion and sharing your vulnerability with someone close to you.

3. Notice how the sharing of emotion lessens the need for control.

Chapter 6:
Moving Forward in the Face of Despair— Fear

If you suffer from fear issues, life feels difficult. You may try to stifle your fears with food, alcohol or addictive substances. You may occupy your mind by watching television or playing video games excessively, working frantically or taking psychoactive medications or sleeping pills.

You may be a serial dater (or marry frequently) because you keep searching for someone who can finally stop your fears; but no one can do that but you, so you keep moving. You have a flight of ideas to keep you safe, but none of them work for long.

When you overcome this fourth challenge, you gain self-esteem and a greater desire to engage with the world. You feel relaxed, stress-free and joyful.

Do you know that a deadly food is hiding in your kitchen pantry?

Have you heard that more people die every year of bird flu than from drunken driving accidents?

Does it bother you that a woman of 45 has a greater chance of being gunned down in the grocery store than of finding a husband?

Do you realize that nothing in the previous paragraph is true?

We are so used to having our fears manipulated, that most of us don't think much about it anymore. Statistics are inflated, bogus comparisons are tossed out and news teasers bombard us every time we turn on the television. These are easy to deal with because we can simply stop listening.

There are also tough fears that are hardwired from childhood experiences, learned by personal experience or influenced by societal norms. Ultimately, we all face the fear of mortality. Some individuals are preoccupied with death years before it is likely, but a generally fearful person expects a certain demise on a number of levels every day—demise of confidence, of self-worth and eventually of one's body.

Some people flick fear away like dandruff. Others let it take root, grow, and flower into full-blown panic. As you might imagine, it is impossible to feel free if you have a garden of fear keeping you emotionally paralyzed.

The amount of fear you have is reflected in your lack of faith in yourself. There are appropriate times to feel fearful—late at night when you hear a window break on the other side of the house. But fearful people also experience fear in situations of conflict or uncertainty because they don't believe they have the personal resources to succeed. Is it any wonder that public speaking is the single most common fear?

Fear grows when it is left in the dark. You have to uproot it. When you don't deal with your fears, you have to use defenses to cover them up. This takes energy. Over time, you just pile a series of defensive structures on top of each other.

Eventually, you can't even find yourself amid the distraction and exhaustion of fear and defenses. That is why some people have trouble being alone. It is part of the reason people overeat, take drugs or drink alcohol to excess.

When we are alone, we think; and if we are afraid of what might come to the surface, we stuff it back into place with mind-altering substances. So we try not to be alone with our thoughts. That's how fear keeps us stuck—it destroys our ability to dream, to plan, to act, to love.

This chapter explores the fourth challenge—fear—through the lens of psychological defenses and spirituality. It talks about the root causes—how some fears are hardwired from childhood experiences, some are learned through experience, and others are influenced by social norms.

Unless we can overcome this challenge, we live in constant emotional turmoil. I describe the process of overcoming fear through the examples of three clients—Olivia, a woman who has struggled with the fear of being unwanted most of her life; and Michael and Lori, a married couple whose lives took divergent spiritual courses when their son died in a bike accident.

Michael and Lori posed these questions to me upon our first meeting, "How can you lose a child to a freak accident and not be fearful for the rest of your life? How can you trust in a God who would allow your youngest to die needlessly while riding a bike on a seldom traveled cul-de-sac? How can you live and not expect the worst? Every time something good happens, won't you expect tragedy to follow? If you lose faith in the afterlife, can life have meaning?"

Little did they know I had visited these questions before, both personally and as a professional. The worst tragedy I can imagine is to lose a child; paralysis is my second fear and as you know from the previous chapter, I have been witness to individuals conquering both of these tragedies.

As I listened to Michael and Lori, it seemed different, however. Their son was an all-star little league baseball player, an outstanding student, an altar boy and was loved by many in his extended family and community. He was riding his bike on their little street when a truck carrying gravel turned around the corner.

It was beginning to rain and the driver didn't see the little boy turning toward him. The side of his truck clipped Jimmy and his bike, and he died instantly as he hit the pavement. The driver reportedly still suffers from deep depression, guilt and was hospitalized psychiatrically six months after the accident.

Michael and Lori actually visited the driver in the hospital. They couldn't bear to have him suffer any longer without letting him know they did not blame him for the tragedy.

The police told them that, in their opinion, the accident was not due to negligence of the driver. The wheels of the truck slid with the wet pavement and the corner was a very sharp turn. It is quite possible that because Jimmy was so tiny, the driver just didn't see him as he attempted to negotiate the corner.

Where is My God?

Michael had attended seminary as a young man, hoping to be ordained a Catholic priest. He eventually became disenchanted with his studies and transferred to Boston College where he felt he could continue to study theology but would not have to commit to the priesthood.

When he and Lori met, she was very attracted to his strong faith. She believed they were an unusual match as very few classmates, even at a Catholic college, seemed so close to God and her faith.

In the beginning of their marriage, this perspective continued. After having children they took both sons to church every Sunday. Lori taught religious studies, and life seemed exactly as they had planned. Michael found a job as a journalist for a small publisher after graduation and Lori taught first grade at a school in their hometown.

They were viewed as an ideal family, devoting much time to the church and belonging to several committees. Michael even found the time to coach Jimmy's little league baseball team. Younger brother, Brian, would tag along to practices and games, functioning as a water boy and hoping to play on his big brother's team someday. At the time of the accident Jimmy was nine and his brother was seven.

Ironically, my cousin and his wife lived on the same street as Michael and Lori, so I was very familiar with the tragedy. After hearing how involved and caring they had been to their community I prayed that some way, somehow I could be of help to them.

I continued to pray for this opportunity and a few years after the accident I received a phone call from Michael. He and Lori came to our first session together and the questions flowed readily. They both cried as they talked about the accident and she sobbed so uncontrollably it was hard for me to keep my composure.

At a certain point in the session, they were not talking so much about the death of their son. They were talking about their marriage falling apart. Lori had turned to the church for solace and Michael had rejected the church altogether. She couldn't believe that at this most critical time he would turn away from God. "All your training, all you told me when we were dating. Now something goes wrong and you lose your faith completely."

Michael did not respond for some time; he was so devastated, his thinking seemed to be in slow motion, often the case with major depressions. He mustered up the courage to utter one deeply profound comment, "How could your God, our God, or any God allow a young innocent boy to be struck and killed? Tell me how a God of kindness and compassion can allow such a thing."

They would debate back and forth, but it was clear: Lori was drawn closer to her church, and Michael was moving farther away each day. It was at this juncture that I suggested Michael join one of my group sessions. I had a hunch that Michael may not be able to restore his faith in God, an entity he could not touch or see, but I thought he might be able to regain his faith in human beings and ultimately in himself.

You've got to Have Faith

Michael's entrance into the group process was difficult for him. He later admitted, "I was trying to play the role of the good group member at first. Then I realized as I began to trust people more and more, that I was getting nowhere by pretending. When I decided to tell them about Jimmy; that is when I started to feel like I belonged."

Members had actually wondered why Michael was attending—he seemed sensitive and quite bright, didn't have difficulty putting his thoughts into words. His mood was low, but people thought that was just his personality.

One night the topic turned to fear. One member talked of his fear of losing his mother since she had had a stroke recently. Another member talked of his mom being diagnosed with early stage Alzheimer's. He was very close to his mother and not only feared her demise but wondered if he would be a candidate for the illness.

One woman talked of being 37, single and never married. She feared that she would grow old alone. Her very worst fear was that she may never have her own child. Lastly, one of the male members talked of his fear for his relationship with his young son. He had divorced and his ex-wife moved to Connecticut, a two hour drive. She had moved in with her boyfriend and he feared for his son's development and wondered how he was going to possibly remain close with such distance.

Michael began to tear at this point. "Don't worry. As long as he is alive and you make the effort, you will be close to him. He will know you care."

Immediately someone asked what he meant by saying "as long as he is alive." "What a depressing thought," one woman uttered.

Michael replied, "Not as depressing as actually losing a son," and the story slowly unfolded.

No one could hold back tears; all the men were misty and the woman were either crying or just trying not to sob or interrupt Michael from speaking. He cried as he struggled with each sentence.

He didn't tell all the details that night—that came later—but he had begun. He had begun to connect to the human race again. He was feeling his own pain and he could see the deep concern others felt for him. He has lost his church, but he was regaining a sense of community in a different form.

He came back the next week and said, "This was the first week that I didn't wake with cold sweats, or feared going to sleep. I actually slept a few more hours without being afraid I wouldn't wake up."

For Michael, one kind of faith had been replaced by another. In the process, fear had somewhat dissipated.

Belief and Doubt

Michael subsequently started to regain some of the belief in himself that had been shattered as a result of his son's death. He has always been somewhat reticent around people. Growing up in a highly educated family with constant oversight, Michael felt inhibited to speak at the risk of being corrected. Even now he still hears his mother saying, "You're using improper grammar, poor choice of words, etc."

His two older sisters excelled academically and Michael was branded "the dreamer" by his mother, meaning he always seemed to be trying to find the meaning in things, not simply being satisfied with obtaining an "A."

His early teachers labeled him eccentric, not beating to the more familiar drum of his classmates. He had frequent questions for his teachers. He would frustrate them since he would daydream often and read only what interested him, rather than doing assigned homework.

This pattern continued through high school. His parents threatened to send him to a residential school, but he managed to perform enough in his junior year that they became resigned to let him finish high school in his hometown.

Michael was involved in a church youth group and he formed a close relationship with a young priest from Ireland that he still treasures today. Michael's Irish-Catholic, extended family had several members who had become priests over the years. He adopted the view that priests were free to help people and study social issues that he knew would be of interest to him. He also had a very special feeling while being on the altar on Sunday mornings as an altar boy.

In retrospect, Michael realized his interest in being a priest was an attempt to be free to understand and learn about God and to be exposed to great teachers like his parish priest. He also became aware that this choice protected him from his anxiety about women. "I just never felt quite comfortable to ask a girl out or even to let anyone know I had a crush. I always expected rejection."

He also believed he would get his mother off his back by entering the priesthood. "I knew she would leave me alone for a while if she could tell the relatives I was attending seminary." Once he began his studies, he became steadily disappointed, finding Catholicism too rigid and dogmatic. Older priests seemed so certain of their beliefs and, unlike him, they didn't appear willing to entertain perspectives other than their own. He had hoped for more freedom of thought but to his dismay, this was not his experience.

He left the seminary after one year and transferred to Boston College, where he met Lori in a class on world religions. He felt comfortable with her. She was easy to talk to and they shared common beliefs. In her, he found someone who was not threatened by discussing various aspects of faith and spirituality. As a result, he was able to overcome his fear of women. She was non-threatening and her interest in him made steps toward intimacy easier than he had ever anticipated.

Ironically, the shared religious beliefs that cemented their relationship early on became, after Jimmy's death, an area of dispute that made divorce seem a likely option. There is an old saying, "True faith comes from doubt." Michael's doubts were threatening Lori's belief system to the point that his thoughts were accentuating her fears rather than helping soothe them.

A Tragic Opportunity

In order to live without inordinate fear, you must have faith in yourself on a very deep level. You cannot develop and maintain faith in yourself alone; it must be reinforced by validating relationships.

Unfortunately, tragedy strikes most lives at some point, and if we have not nurtured our relationships, we are seldom resilient enough to cope. Resilient people maintain a regular social network and believe they can influence the events in their lives. They accept change as a challenge that can produce greater satisfaction in life, as opposed to perceiving change as a threat that cannot be overcome.

In essence, they believe regrets can be altered by current behavior. Tragedy is not a requested opportunity, but a time to find out who we really are, what we really believe in, and where we find meaning. One of my clients calls these times in life a tragetunity.

How would these two suffering parents resolve their fundamental differences? We met in couples' sessions and talked about their various views, their disappointment in each other and often we would struggle to find the common ground between them.

The common ground eventually became the point of focus. Both were afraid to live again, they had fear of losing their youngest son. They had become overprotective and were also worrying about their aging parents. Lori remarked one night, "I can't tolerate another death, I can't bear another funeral. I just want to stop thinking of caskets and sorrow."

Coping with the Loss

Michael and Lori were trying valiantly to find a way to cope. Lori fell back on her traditional beliefs. Michael believed he had become more spiritual and less religious. His joining group sessions created a different kind of group for him, and ultimately, he came to call it his "learning group."

"My experience in group has not just helped me bear Jimmy's death; it has made me a better person. I understand people better. I can communicate with less self-criticism and most importantly, I learned that if I can be real and expose my soul, my fears dissipate. This didn't happen all at once, it has taken much work, but I have regained my interest in life. I don't feel as afraid anymore."

Michael had developed a belief in the spirit of relationships. "I'm amazed how a group of strangers can get together, talk openly with your help and, in the end, emerge from pain and stress as stronger people." Lori held this belief also. It was not being in church alone that gave her a feeling of relief; it was seeing all those caring faces that stayed with her every step of the way— people who listened and gave her hope when she was most fearful.

Her faith was critical, but human beings provided the solace she needed and thrived on. Michael felt similarly. It was difficult for Lori to accept Michael's loss of faith in a "higher power" but she certainly understood his focus on the spirit-giving relationships in his life. She knew she could not emerge whole without the touch and words of those closest to her.

There is an old story that reportedly originated in an AA meeting years ago regarding a debate between a priest, a minister and a rabbi. They were talking about the differences between religion and spirituality. After listening to all three go on and on for an hour an "old timer" got up and asked to speak, "I don't know why the three of you are making such a big deal out of this. It's pretty simple: religious people are those who are afraid of going to hell; those of us spiritual people have already been there and come back."

Fearless Living

Today Michael and Lori have made many changes, many compromises and have taken risks they would not have considered if tragedy had not struck their lives.

They have also chosen new directions in their careers. They decided, after much sorrow and pain, to move forward in life with passion and creativity. They have lost their old self-consciousness and are less concerned with pleasing others at their own sacrifice.

Lori had struggled with her weight since her first pregnancy, never being able to exercise or eat healthily with consistency. Before working on her nutrition and developing an exercise routine, I focused on her resistance to taking better care of herself. It turns out she had secretly resented Michael from the time of her second pregnancy. She had gained considerable weight and she believed this turned him off. Her proof was that he seldom approached her romantically and their sex life was almost non-existent.

Her private theory contributed to her low mood, fueling her desire for simple carbohydrates, which in turn left little energy to exercise. This cycle continued until we examined the reality of her theory.

Michael vehemently denied that he was not attracted to Lori, but he did assert that her constant complaining about her weight and the constant negativity aired in front of young Brian was a complete turn off. "You complain out loud every time you put a dress on but you refuse to exercise or do anything constructive to solve the problem."

She couldn't deny his account and she was, in fact, relieved to hear his reasoning.

Ultimately, both she and Michael decided they wanted to live in a more vibrant manner. They reminded me that they had a son who needed them to be as healthy as possible. He didn't need to worry about his parents, accentuating his fear of the future. He was already struggling with missing his brother and wondering if he really was in Heaven. They bought a treadmill and started taking long walks on weekends together

(an example of another compromise reached by two individuals who viewed each other as unbending weeks ago.)

As a result of their mutual courage and dedication to growing as individuals, they have a direction in their lives not previously felt. They are more intimate with each other, and are having a sexual connection deeper than ever before. None of these changes came easily, but as fear dissipated, they grew emotionally. They were enormously fearful after the accident, but today they have little time to ponder what could go wrong because they are preoccupied with what is going right.

Interestingly, Michael and Lori's charged arguments about religion, initially causing much consternation, ultimately brought them a new-found respect for each other. Rather than religious differences creating a war, it created a need to respect an alternative point of view. In the final analysis, they found commonality in their beliefs.

They found this conflict difficult to navigate initially and then dis-covered that the one aspect they have in common is a new definition and experience of love. They have come to experience a deeper love for each other, a love that has grown to new heights based on the faith that they can work through even the most tragic of circumstances; a love based on knowing each other as they are and not as they wish each other to be; a love based on uncritical affection; a love that does not yield to fear, but moves forward despite life's circumstances.

One of the greatest fears people have in our culture today is loss of love.

Fearful Love—Olivia's Story

Olivia, age 42, came to the states from England after her daughter gradu-ated from college not very long ago. Her first marriage ended in divorce after four years when her husband had an affair and ultimately left Olivia and her daughter.

She remarried Ralph, a 62-year-old businessman two years before she moved to the states. He has two adult sons by a first marriage. Olivia is an attractive, well-educated woman who impresses with her quick wit and intelligence. She met Ralph while both were working in London, he as a stock analyst and she as a buyer for women's attire.

She grew up in the country as the oldest of four girls. She describes her father as "almost paranoid." He had few friends, many eccentric quirks and cautioned all his children to be very careful not to take risks in life. His motto was to stay with whatever is familiar. He worked in the same machine shop for over thirty-five years, despite other more advantageous opportunities. His social skills were quite limited and Olivia's mother handled most of the parental duties—attending school functions, plays, etc.

Her mother was a very dependent woman who feared venturing out too far on her own and would only attend Sunday church if a neighbor drove her (despite the fact that the church was only a mile away.) Her mother frequently complained to Olivia about her husband and men in general.

Olivia called for a consultation as she had become depressed in America, disappointed it was not what Ralph predicted. He wanted to get away from his children and ex-wife and believed the opportunities were vast here in the states.

Money is very important to Ralph and he often talked of how their combined income would provide a glorious life for both of them. Olivia was laid off from her first job after six months. Ralph was overly upset about the loss of income. He nevertheless managed to purchase an expensive sports car during this time and other toys for home entertainment.

Olivia is now working again, traveling weekly and Ralph is happy again that their financial picture looks bright. In fact, they have plenty of money, but Ralph has always had insecurity about income (a bit of performance addiction here—money equals love and respect and unfortunately Olivia feels quite responsible for pleasing Ralph.)

The difference in their ages is an issue as he is approaching retirement and is increasingly worried that they won't be able to maintain their current lifestyle. He has told her in my presence that he expects her "to carry the load for the foreseeable future."

Olivia feels depressed about her plight, but she seldom addresses Ralph. "Does he love me or does he say he loves me because I can earn what he desires?"

She always worries that people will leave her if she addresses any of her differences with them and this fear is not limited to Ralph.

When she calls home, she reacts similarly with her parents, always fearing loss of their love if she asserts her own wishes.

Many times she does not seem to know what she wants in life. She is frequently trying to discern cues from others as to what they want, what will please them and what will protect the fragile love she believes they have for her.

Olivia was an ideal candidate for a group coaching experience as she would have the opportunity to change this damaging hardwiring by addressing her fears directly. Her anxieties were created interpersonally and I thought they could be undone the same way. She clearly needed to learn to assert herself with others, but this challenge would be a momentous undertaking for her. Nevertheless, she was willing to forge ahead.

Despite her fear of losing affection from others, Olivia is a very courageous woman. She will persevere, especially when she feels those guiding her are trustworthy and consistent. We had developed a very positive connection and I knew she trusted my judgment as to what might benefit her.

Neuroscientists have proven that when human beings feel safe and secure, we produce the hormone oxytocin, a hormone which gives a feeling of warmth and closeness to others. When people have this experience, they are much more likely to express directly. Olivia has been a poster child for this experience.

Olivia began group with much reservation. She was extremely anxious, trying to entertain people, making sure she was pleasing everyone and not objecting to anything or anyone.

To her surprise her efforts were not working well with group members. She received feedback that at first upset her, but ultimately propelled her into an emotional growth spurt.

Bob, one of our more sensitive members, tactfully addressed her one night. "Olivia, I know what you're doing 'cause I do the same thing all the time. You're so afraid of losing people's approval that you reveal very little about yourself. It's as if you're not here for yourself, you're here to make us all happy. You're always trying to make sure there is no conflict, no objections, it's all safe talk."

She was hurt that evening, she had tears at the end of the meeting but came back the next week and began to reveal more. She told us of her fragile sense of self, how she doubted whether her own parents really loved her, revealed her doubts about her marriage and described her overall fears of being rejected by people.

One of the group members commented, "What is she to do? We have learned that Olivia is hardwired to believe that people will react to her like her parents did. She can't trust and expects people to abandon her. So what is the answer for her?"

Another member commented, "I am so amazed. We're all capable, intelligent people, but not one of us feels comfortable in our own skin. I want to know what Olivia can do and what we can all do to change."

I replied by saying, "What we all need to do is to find out the truth of our own story. We all come into adulthood with biases. We need to learn the absolute truth about who we are and, through this group process we are all committed to doing so. For instance, is it true that Olivia has to be as careful as she is with people? Are all adults rejecting like her father? Do people only love us if we perform for them the way they want? Is love that superficial, that fickle? Spiritual learners have the courage to find out, from all credible sources, what truth is for them and for others."

Sharon Begley, in her insightful book Train Your Mind, Change Your Brain, examines the fascinating research of many psychologists, neuro-scientists and, with the help of the Dalai Lama, the minds of Tibetan monks. This research proves that new experiences change the brain, and situations that improve emotional security reduce prejudice and bias.

I would add that this phenomenon includes self-biases. One evening, as Olivia attended a group session after returning from a trip back home to England, a profound change took place. It is an example of how a behavioral change causes a neurochemical change that reverses old hardwiring.

Olivia had been criticized in group for always trying to be so pleasing, constantly apologizing for her style of communication and often making self-depreciating comments. One reason Olivia is programmed this way is that it reduces her fear of criticism. How? She criticizes herself before anyone else has a chance to do so.

Brent, one of our more aggressive and truthful members, found her style irritating. He was after her to "just say what you think; stop trying to be so nice; spit it out." Olivia had been away for three weeks and upon her return, Brent began group talking about some matters that had been of concern to him in his commercial real estate business. Neither he nor others asked Olivia how her trip went.

They knew she was quite anxious about seeing her parents and brothers as she had been in conflict with them over the phone recently. She had discussed her dismay about her family in group before she returned to England, yet no one took the time to inquire. Once again, she felt rejected and abandoned.

As the group went on, I could tell she was becoming irritated. I asked what she was experiencing and she initially deflected, but in a moment, catching herself doing the same old thing, she changed direction. "You all want me to say what I think, to stop avoiding conflict and just spit it out. Well okay, I feel like spitting at you, Brent. You dominate each meeting with the same old stuff; it's always about you. You complain about your employees, your wife and your daughter. We're all supposed to sit and devote our attention to you each week. You don't even bother to ask me about my trip, in fact, none of you have. I think you're all a bunch of self-centered hypocrites."

I had never seen Olivia as angry as she was that evening. I could see when she finished, she was tempted to take back her remarks, but she held firm. Brent apologized in a half-hearted way and she came right back at him again. "You're just saving face now. You really don't care about me and don't pretend that you do."

Others apologized but were unclear as to why they didn't ask her about her trip. Group ended and the following week a member immediately asked Olivia how she felt after she left the preceding week. "I felt guilty at first, but then I realized I have held back my true feelings all my life, always fearful people would leave me. Well, if you all want me to leave group, I would rather leave than go on pretending."

Joyce, a member who also has difficulties expressing directly without feeling guilty, told Olivia she felt closer to her since the previous week. She said she thought hard as to why she had not asked about her trip. "I don't mean to blame you, Olivia, but I knew if I asked, it would be like pulling teeth to get the real answer. You always try so hard to make everything seem so rosy, that it does get frustrating to pull things out of you. Last week you were so direct, clear and to the point. I felt like a cheerleader in your corner and I realized I need to learn to come forward also."

One by one each group member told Olivia of how refreshing it was to hear her be so direct, so passionate about what she felt with no apologies. Olivia got the response she had never anticipated. Rather than people responding as her father, who didn't allow any discourse in the family, group members responded in a way that indicated they felt more connected.

Olivia began a process that night that has continued in all aspects of her life. She has been more direct with her husband, family, friends and coworkers. You can see the vibrancy in her face. She no longer looks forlorn and burdened. I believe that on some level she felt enough support in the group that she was able to come forward without the same level of fear she had experienced so often.

She changed her neurochemistry through relating in a different manner. When we release stress hormones, they work against our attempts to elevate our spirits, which is part of why Olivia no longer feels stressed.

High quality relating is a natural way of protecting our brains and our immune system. Olivia will never forget the night she began an emotional growth spurt that resulted in a more confident, less fearful perspective on life.

Questions to Journal:

Your journal is growing and your story is changing!

Below are a series of questions for you to consider that will help you iden¬tify the role of fear in your life. Try to answer as immediately as you can without rehearsing your answer. In essence, give up some control and your responses will be more revealing. Remember sharing your journal with those close to you is the key to emotional freedom.

- What were your reactions to Michael and Lori's story?

- What aspects of their lives caused you fear?

- We are hardwired to feel secure or fearful in the world very early in life. Who influenced your perspective and how did this learn ing take place?

- Do you feel you're stuck in your old story? Or do you feel you can unlearn the relationship you have to fear through new learning with more objective people?

- In most cases, our images of God are also hardwired early in life. If you believe in God is he/she understanding, punitive, forgiving, dogmatic etc.? What is his/her nature?

- Is whatever you wrote to the previous question a perspective on God that comes from childhood, or is your current position a perspective you came to understand in adulthood?

- What do you think of the idea that true faith comes from having the ability to doubt?

- What is your capacity for tolerating a fundamental difference of opinion with people?

- Do you fear losing status if you acknowledge that someone else's opinion is more accurate than your own?

- Are you fearful to assert your beliefs, values, or desires as it may mean displeasing those close to you?

- If so, how did you learn to perceive in that way?

- To what degree are you fearful that love is dependent upon your performance or your appearance?

- Can you relate to Olivia's journey away from fear and toward assertive expression?

- How often are you too afraid to speak your mind? What people or situations stimulate this behavior?

- When you think of rewriting your story, does it invoke fear? If so, why?

- What are you anticipating will change in your life if you rewrite your novel?

- What are you afraid to give up? Explain.

Get Grounded in Experience:

1. Tell someone close to you what your greatest fear is currently in your life.

2. Ask for help in deciding how real the likelihood of this fear is in influencing your life, and also ask for help in coping if, in fact, it is a fear based in truth (or fallacy.)

Chapter 7:
Learning to Read between the Lines— Intimacy

The fifth trial to happiness and life satisfaction is intimacy. Intimacy is the ability to enter the personal world of another person. Seventy percent of Americans indicate that a "good life" is dependent on their relationships.

At the most basic level, it drives everything we do. Why are we so concerned about the way we look or our status? We chase these qualities because we believe that they will bring us love or respect. The key to conquering this challenge is to discover how to generate intimacy and love from within ourselves, without relying on the crutch of these superficial signifiers.

As important as intimacy is, many of us are remarkably inept at creating or sustaining it. Signs of such intimacy deficits include an inability to 1) manage self-care; 2) communicate assertively and directly; 3) understand mature sexuality; and 4) understand that the self and the other person are interwoven. This chapter examines the most important challenge—intimacy. I use the case example of Scott and Rita, a couple who have everything—money, respect, happy children, a thriving business and an active social life—but they don't have intimacy. Therefore they feel their lives have not been successful.

As is true with most couples, Rita and Scott's problems stem from patterns and psychological issues they had before they ever met each other.

Marriage is a terrific magnifier—whatever is troubling to an individual can be devastating when they bring those problems to a partnership. By addressing their intimacy issues, Scott and Rita have pulled back from the brink of divorce and are stronger individually, in their marriage and within their family.

If you suffer from intimacy problems, you may feel unloved, underappreciated and alone. You probably trust too easily or not enough. You may feel that you don't need anyone or that you don't need to tell people how you feel.

When you overcome this fifth challenge, you gain a greater love of yourself and the ability to love others. All your relationships—family, work, friends—improve. You may discover new closeness with your children, avoid a divorce and reconnect on a very basic level. You become physically and emotionally healthier.

Watch a group of children on any playground and you'll see instant friendships, secret-sharing and complicated play that progresses without spoken rules. That is intimacy. It is natural and effortless in an uncluttered soul.

For adults, intimacy is more difficult. We bring our fears, control issues, expectations, regrets and unrealistic dreams with us (essentially, our entire biased story.) This effectively blocks that simple sharing that comes so easily to children. Intimacy is perhaps the fiercest trial to happiness and life satisfaction. But as important as it is, many of us are remarkably inept at creating or sustaining true intimacy.

Signs of intimacy deficits may be surprising. For example, I'm sure you've heard the old saying that you can't love someone else until you love yourself or at least have an accepting attitude toward yourself. It's true—self-care is the most neglected aspect of loving and caring for someone else.

In addition to psychological wellness, self-care involves eating well; exercising, reducing stress, doing meaningful work and doing all the other things that keep us physically and mentally well. You compromise your ability to care for others properly or enjoy life with another person if you are not healthy. Our inability to care for ourselves can have devastating effects on our partner, close friends and family. It affects all aspects of our lives.

Real intimacy involves truthful exchange of thoughts, ideas, dreams and plans. It means expressing oneself sexually and communicating with your partner about his or her sexual passions.

Aging brings new challenges to our sexual life and it is critical to understand the effects of hormone changes. This area is one of great confusion to most couples. Men, in particular, often personalize their wives' changing libido as peri-menopause and menopause itself can have significant influences. Low testosterone levels for men can also have a dramatic impact, although less common.

Empathy is the key to understanding and maintaining intimacy.

Without empathy, we cannot accurately access another's character—their level of honesty, integrity and responsibility—which defines and refines relationships. Without empathy, we generalize and personalize, often causing unnecessary tension. Empathy gives intimacy strength and sustainability, even in the most trying life circumstances.

Wishing on a Star—Image Love

In long-term love relationships, our hearts can become heavy, causing us to lose the spontaneity we once had. In the beginning, we think we are falling in love with a real person, but the energy of early love is often fueled by expectations and dreams that cannot possibly come true.

Through the experience of Scott and Rita, we will learn how a couple goes from the brink of divorce to a level of intimacy never imagined. Both Rita and Scott came from painful backgrounds. The details may not be necessary to convey.

As Scott has said, "We had all these unpleasant feelings and memories from our past. We met each other, fell in love, thought we had found the cure and dumped all our hurts between us, thinking the other would solve our feelings of inadequacy."

As time went on, the expectations of feeling "whole" disappeared, causing Scott and Rita to blame each other for their discontent. Rita drank more; Scott ate more, and both became unhappy.

Eventually, they were on my doorstep asking for help. He was unhappy with her drinking, and she was unhappy with his significant weight gain and resultant ill health. They both had elevated blood pressure and higher than normal cholesterol levels.

Both had been athletes in high school and continued exercising somewhat in college. Rita played varsity soccer for two years and then moved in with Scott her junior year and quit the team. Now, Rita exercises daily despite her nighttime drinking, but Scott had abandoned working out several years ago, stating the familiar rationale: "I'm too busy with work and other obligations."

Self Care—Other Care

Couples are often surprised when I make the comment that self care dramatically affects the quality of long-term relationships. Our ability or inability to take care of ourselves influences all the significant people in our lives.

Weight and appearance are obviously touchy issues, as the motivation for concern may be based on image love rather than a concern for the health of your partner. For example, when Rita complained about Scott's weight gain, he immediately interpreted her comments as superficial. "You just want me to look like someone you can be proud of. It's all about your ego."

It was difficult for Rita to respond. She had struggled with her weight a significant part of her life and she knew how shallow people can be when it comes to this topic. Even she wondered about her true intent. Was she feeling embarrassed by his "beer belly," or did she really care about his health?

She wanted to grow old with someone who would continue to be physically active. She loved golf, swimming and played in a women's soccer league in the fall. Regardless, her drinking compromised her health. I reminded her of the increased frequency of breast cancer among females, who drank more than a drink daily, and she gave me another familiar excuse, "But I exercise every day."

The resistance and excuses that keep us from forming healthy self-care habits are endless. We have more information regarding nutrition and exercise than any civilized nation, yet we have the highest rates of obesity. Why? Education alone is not enough. Understanding the nature of your sense of self is crucial to self care. If, on the deepest level, you are without faith in yourself, it will manifest in your daily habits.

It doesn't matter how educated, intelligent or how many personal trainers you have. If you don't believe in yourself and your ability to cope with change successfully, you will ultimately falter and your ability to be an intimate partner will also be compromised.

Once conscientious people realize that this struggle not only affects their own identity but is affecting those closest to them, they often begin the process of learning and changing.

Rita and Scott's denial of their own destructive habits was not a product of their marriage. It was a product of the sense of self they have struggled with all their lives. Blaming each other kept them at an impasse. As long as we believe others are responsible for our means of coping, we are stuck in the mud.

It's so easy to adopt this position in a marriage. "If only she made me breakfast, then I'd have time to exercise" or "If he would help out once in a while, I could go for a run."

These complaints are based on our own unique way of coping with marital disappointment. I have often said that one of the unconscious reasons we marry is to have someone to blame for our insecurities, the areas of our lives where we struggle and wish someone else would take charge.

Our coping style was determined long before we ever met our spouse. I recently met with a woman going through a contentious divorce who stated that her time at the gym has been her lifesaver. She had decided to cope in the best way available rather than sit in a rocking chair and blame her soon to be ex-husband for having little energy. Recent research on the positive effects of exercise on depression and anxiety is astounding. Some studies even indicate that aerobic exercise is superior to anti-depressants (refer to the book Spark by Dr. John Ratey for further details.)

Once I was able to expand Scott and Rita's view of their unique way of responding to conflict, and they understood the consequences of their actions, movement toward more balanced health began. Change was especially noticeable when both acknowledged that they were compromising their children's development.

"Will You Still Love Me When I'm..."

The Beatles song about the possibility of losing love as we age is an American worry that permeates many marriages. Scott was testing Rita's love by asking a critical question and she did not have a great answer, (at least her ambiguous reply left him with the excuse to keep eating to spite her for her shallow perspective.)

Turns out, she did care about his health. However, because they had so much friction between them, it didn't come across until we worked out many of their suppressed resentments.

We tend to focus on the superficial when trust is lost. If we don't feel heard or special to our spouse, feelings become bitter and the slightest offense can cause an intense reaction.

Rita and Scott were incredibly irritable with each other. I commented one evening that they treat me better than they treat each other, even after I make a critical comment. I could give the exact same feedback that caused an argument between them and they would respond with understanding.

They had little training in how to manage conflict. Both had poor role models growing up and were at a loss as to how to resolve differences constructively. As intelligent and capable people, this dilemma baffled both of them.

As many capable people do, they thought that intelligence alone should be enough to solve dilemmas between them. Because they gave little credence to emotional hardwiring, it took considerable time for them to grasp and admit that they needed guidance and coaching in this emotional area.

I Can't Hear You

Rita and Scott had felt so rejected by each other for so long that they seldom listened from an open position. One would talk and the other's eyes would roll or a deep breath would indicate disapproval. They took the familiar position that there was nothing they hadn't heard from the other before. The old saying that familiarity breeds contempt would apply to both of them. The erroneous assumption that once we have lived with someone for a considerable amount of time we know all about them is a dangerous perspective to maintain.

Scott's interpretation of Rita's view of his weight is an excellent example. He was not aware that his worst fear was that her love was exclusively based on image. He had self-hatred for his inability to manage his body. He despised himself for turning to emotional eating to cope with life stressors.

Rita was amazed to realize that, as she became closer to Scott, because of our work together, she found him more attractive, even though he had lost little weight. Her previous perceptions had been skewed by her feelings of rejection. She was surprised how deeply she felt for him, even though she seldom felt special to him. She soothed her sense of rejection by drinking wine at night.

In essence Scott's individual struggle was exacerbated as the marriage became more distant and feelings of specialness were greatly diminished. Both felt unloved by the other and nothing could have been farther from the truth.

In order for their hearts to be revealed, they needed to stop assuming and start learning about each other.

Chapter Headlines

Upon initially meeting Rita, Scott thought he was pretty sure what type of woman she was. He said, "After all, I knew she grew up in a rich town. Her father was an attorney and mother was a business woman. She played soccer and was in a top sorority."

These are what I call *chapter headlines*. They give us a glimmer of the content of a book or of a life, but not much else. Some people, either because their longings are so strong or because they have little faith in their ability to access another, will be lead by *chapter headlines* to their detriment.

Rita, on the other hand, saw Scott as a "tall Lutheran from Minnesota, laid back, star baseball player who wouldn't hurt a flea."

I always ask couples about their very first impression of each other. These perceptions often tell a story that forecasts hidden difficulties.

Scott was attracted to an image, a person who could raise his status. He felt inhibited as a country boy from a small Midwestern town. He told me in the first interview that he was not cultured like Rita, "My parents are simple people, good people, but not at all exposed to the world like Rita's folks."

Rita, on the other hand, liked the fact that Scott seemed so at ease with just "hanging out. He seemed so comfortable just being, didn't have all those performance expectations I grew up with."

Isn't it interesting that often what we initially appreciate in a relationship, we can ultimately dislike?

In the early therapy sessions, Scott complained that Rita thought she was better than other people. "She talks down to people. So what if her parents are big shots?" Rita, on the other hand, has grown tired of Scott's laid back work habits. "He just doesn't seem to really want to make more of himself. He could have been a VP by now if he'd pushed."

They read the cover of this love story, skimmed *chapter headlines*, but missed the deepest content of the story. Psychotherapy offered them the hope of actually coming to know each other on a more accurate level and to see if this "knowing" could re-stimulate love and prevent the divorce they were contemplating.

A Story Untold

As we began to unravel their difficulties, it became clear that much of what they blamed each other for had already existed in each of their lives. Scott was right; they dumped all their hurts and unresolved past issues into the middle of the marriage. Then they unconsciously expected the other to soothe the emotional pains of the past.

Rather than doing the work to re-write their stories, they expected the other to simply soothe their historical hurts and change their view of themselves with a love potion that erased their childhood.

As I mentioned before, one of the unconscious reasons people marry is to have someone to blame, someone to hold responsible for their vulnerabilities, fears and insecurities. Many of us realize along the way that this wish is unfair. In healthy relationships people focus less on expectations of the other and more on one's own growth.

Scott and Rita fell in love quickly as soon as they had experienced the binding and blinding effects of passionate sex. They thought they had experienced nirvana and all would be well.

Sex is enormously deceiving in that physical closeness and the neurochemical changes that accompany sex can make us think we really know someone. Soon thereafter, the real process of loving began. As with many wistful romances, it went well for Scott and Rita—until they had children.

Our new emerging families bring back memories of our earlier family experiences. Every developmental phase our children encounter reminds us of the same period of our lives. Freud reportedly stated there are only two ways we can overcome neurosis—go into analysis or have a baby.

Children force us to reflect and remember the many experiences we have put away in the recesses of our minds. Parenting gives us an ongoing opportunity to gain insight into our past through our children. We get another view of the story we created and have another opportunity to examine its validity.

As time goes by, we slowly discover the real person we married. The image of the person we were hoping for, the one, who would cure our ills and make us whole, has disappeared and soon after this period, disappointment sets in.

It has been said that, on our wedding night, there are at least six people in the wedding bed—mother, father, bride; mother, father, groom; and possibly several others. We bring our history and all our conditioning (positive and negative) to the present. We look to our newfound love to resolve our past, but it can't happen and many can't accept this reality.

Those of us who fail to attain the deepest level of intimacy often blame our partner, feel victimized and either divorce or act out our disappointment through drinking, drugging, affairs, excessive work and other avoidant lifestyles.

Recently Scott visited his elderly, ill mother and Rita began visiting her father before he died shortly thereafter of a terminal illness. They had both been estranged from their parents and with my encouragement, decided to face them before it was too late.

They returned to the "scene of the crime" to see if some degree of resolution could be attained. Neither parent knew why they had suddenly been contacted. These visits didn't produce any deep conversations, but both Scott and Rita, in their own way, faced the origin of their insecurities and came away with greater compassion and forgiveness. They began to see their parents in a different light, as insecure people themselves who possessed limited interpersonal tools.

Scott commented, "Since I have learned how to relate differently, I could see how limited my mother really is. I don't think she knows how to talk about feelings or anything very personal." Rita experienced something similar with her father, "You can see in his eyes he cares. He wants to say something, but it just doesn't come out. Then he ends up asking questions about the presidential race."

Rather than feeling injured, they had begun expanding their empathy to understand the root of each parent's responses or lack of response. We couldn't possibly attain this level of insight as a child, but we have a new opportunity as adults.

As they were able to put their accumulated resentments for each other aside, they learned more about the depth of hurt each had carried forward into the marriage. They became more compassionate with each other, realizing on a more emotional level, how difficult it is to change behaviors you have been exposed to most of your life.

Neither Rita nor Scott had been validated in a direct, constructive manner, so they had little idea of how to give what they never received.

They gained a newfound appreciation for expressing in a tactful, direct manner. They were abandoning old habits through understanding. They had the courage to try new behaviors and actions that they had previously considered too vulnerable to risk.

It's in His Kiss

I remember one evening when I asked them if they kiss. They immediately seemed anxious. Eventually Scott responded, "We had sex like bandits when we first met, but it's funny. I don't remember kissing for long. As time went on, we resorted to giving the perfunctory kiss as we left in the morning, but that's about it."

Rita said that it was too uncomfortable now. She wasn't sure why, but thought it would almost be "like starting all over." As we talked about the intimacy of a passionate kiss, Scott realized he was too angry to kiss Rita. "I just have so much resentment built up; I can't imagine really kissing you."

That comment was the beginning of this couple forming a more intense relationship; not a relationship built on sex alone, but one where old and new conflicts would be worked out so that intimacy could survive. They couldn't kiss with passion because of all the misunderstandings and misinterpretations that had plagued them for years.

They were finally willing to honestly address the many unresolved conflicts between them. Being direct, although initially threatening, allowed for a new beginning. They had the courage to unravel the past, come to a new understanding and move forward.

Slowly, but surely, they began to be more affectionate, as each resentment was resolved or at least understood, it freed up energy for intimacy. One night I saw them both walk into the waiting room holding hands; a pretty remarkable occasion considering that months earlier they were only speaking through their attorneys.

Rita and Scott's story of resolving their past hurts involves courageous action and as each addressed their own frailties, they developed empathy for each other. They began to personalize less, assume less and they began to listen from an open perspective. These efforts on both their parts, led to a deeper understanding of each other.

Rather than being stuck in unrealistic expectations that only led to profound disappointments, they became grounded in the truth of what they can realistically expect from each other. In essence, they fell in love with each other's character rather than a mythical belief system.

They knew that the longings they had before they met had blinded them upon first meeting each other. As Scott and Rita learned, longings create blind spots—we feel satisfied in the immediate and disappointed in the long run. They had the diligence and fortitude to admit their misperceptions and take responsibility for their own unrealistic expectations.

They came to realize that they will always be "getting to know each other." Nothing is etched in stone regarding the human psyche. We are always changing and evolving if we are growing emotionally.

I wrote in *The Power of Empathy* that we touch bodies when we have sex, but we can only touch hearts and souls with empathy guiding the way.

Rita and Scott touched each other's soul and in the process they also touched my soul. They are a constant reminder to me of how human beings can transform themselves and their relationships if they have the courage to be a *spiritual learner*.

Every time I sit with a young person searching for love, I listen for the blind spots, the unrecognized longings that caused Rita and Scott so much discomfort and pain. The next story provides a window into a familiar longing of a somewhat different nature.

Distant Lover

Gina is a 34-year-old woman who has had a history of relationships with men who cannot or will not commit. She often ends up pursuing men who have shown her much initial interest, but as time goes on, give her one excuse or another as to why they had to cancel a date, didn't tell her about the other girlfriend or any other of a number of excuses. Gina seldom de-invests in men that clearly have little capacity for intimacy.

Gina came to me because she had been struggling with depression due to a recent relationship she entered. She felt very dissatisfied, but couldn't bring herself to end it. The man in question had a girlfriend, but told her they'd grown apart. He was going to end the relationship soon, because he was so very attracted to Gina.

Ten months went by and Ray was still singing the same song. He was still involved with the other woman and still calling Gina at 10 or 11 at night, after a night on the town with his buddies, asking if he could come over. Of course she would say yes, against her better judgment. She would then "feel his love" in bed and would continually fall for the next version of the same old play. Over time, I helped Gina de-invest in this relationship only to learn she had begun another of a similar nature.

Gina is the oldest of three girls. Her mother tended to be quite deferential to her father and quite critical of Gina in particular. Her dad was a rather aloof man. He loved to spend time alone working on wood projects in the basement. He made it clear to the family that after work and on weekends, he preferred solitary activities. He worked for a local electric company for many years, had few friends and basically kept to himself most of the time.

Gina saw little affection between her parents, and at age 34, she is the only remaining unmarried sister. She describes both her sisters as having unhealthy marriages. "I would hate to be in their shoes. They are completely controlled by their self-centered husbands."

Her sisters have young children and Gina takes great joy in being their aunt, but also is scared to think she may never have children of her own. She is a professional woman, the only one to graduate college in her immediate and extended family. Nevertheless, she laments, "I would give up my career tomorrow to have my own child. It's really all I want in life and I'm afraid I will be an old spinster who will never be called Mom."

Programmed for Disaster

Gina reluctantly joined one of my group-coaching sessions. We had discussed the possibility for several weeks, but she always felt too anxious to take the risk. One week, after another familiar breakup, she told me she wanted to join—ready or not. I told Gina that the patterns people engage in outside of group over time will manifest themselves in group. For instance, if you traditionally adopt a passive role in relationships then feel resentful that other people seem to dominate; this pattern will be repeated in a group experience.

Gina began group by adopting a very pleasing style, making sure to not say anything controversial about anyone. Several male and female members had initially adopted this style so it was immediately recognizable to them.

One member, after a few meetings, told Gina that he wondered how personal she could actually become in an intimate relationship. She was surprised by this comment and asked for an explanation. "I just wonder if you can ever give up the 'good girl' routine and actually say what you think."

Gina was surprised as this comment was not made in anger. It was made by a member she respected and knew cared for her. He, also single, was trying to tell her that her pleasing behavior was not that pleasing to someone who wanted a deep, honest connection.

Shortly thereafter, as she was trying to be more forthcoming, she mentioned her attraction to one of the group members, a man who admittedly wanted nothing to do with a woman at this particular stage of his life. They would banter back and forth before group and Gina had developed a "crush" on a man that was the least available in group.

Some of the other single males commented that they would have been thrilled if she had found them attractive. Steve, a 42-year-old divorced engineer said, "I would carry you away to the parking lot and keep driving if you said that to me, yet you picked the one person who shows the least interest. I guess you're in the right place, Gina."

This experience ultimately provided Gina with a live example of how she ends up getting involved with men. She picked a man who likes to spend time alone, is rather awkward interpersonally and is not particularly comfortable validating others.

She was returning to the scene of the crime, trying to resolve her relationship with her father, trying to rewrite her story through a man who seemed similar to her dad (thus in her mind, being the kind of man who could help her recreate the past.) She would finally gain the affection and love from a remote type of man, solving the problem by recreating the same type of relationship with a different outcome.

She had never seen this pattern so clearly before. She was embarrassed at first, thinking her behavior was clear to everyone else but her. This live enactment of her story provided Gina with much needed insight into her motivations. This emotional experience made an invaluable impression upon her, one that eventually led to her having the fortitude to take a different tact with men.

I continually reiterate in group that we are all too subjective to see ourselves accurately. We need the feedback of people who see us from a more objective perspective. In a constructive group, we come to an objective consensus over time.

Too Close Too Fast

Recently Gina came in to group with excitement—a man was really pursuing her for a change. He was quite a bit older, but he wrote to her on Match.com and they began a dialogue. They then met for lunch and she saw him five consecutive days after that. "He is so persistent, always calling, texting, wanting to see me every night. I am wondering if this could be real or if this guy has a problem."

Group members encouraged Gina to have an open heart; "Don't make hasty judgments." It was unclear to some whether Gina was uncomfortable with being the one pursued, or if this man was acting in a needy, desperate manner.

As time went on, she began to enjoy the attention more and more, but as they became more involved, he became more possessive. He didn't like her going out for a drink after work on Fridays, didn't see why she had to have dinner with her girlfriends and didn't appreciate her going to a Red Sox game with her sisters. She became increasingly uncomfortable and eventually did something quite uncharacteristic.

She went to his home and told him she didn't want to hurt him, but she didn't think he really cared for her as much as he needed someone to care for and possess. He got very angry. She went home and he left voice messages and emails for several days, insulting her and cursing her for being immature and self-centered. She de-invested from him; set clear limits and didn't feel guilty in the process.

"I loved the attention at first (I seldom have men fuss all over me,) but I realized it was longings getting in the way of reality again. I either pick men who can't commit or need to be committed." Gina didn't feel blue after this encounter.

She is beginning to feel more confident with men, beginning to understand her worth as group members value her in a manner that she is unaccustomed to. She is beginning to digest their feedback as truth. She sees that when she is tactfully assertive, she is respected, not rejected. I am certain that, in time, she will find herself in a romantic relationship unlike any she has experienced to date.

Gina, akin to Rita and Scott, has opened the door to intimacy by having the courage to face the truth of her history. As we have discussed, we have all written our novel with a biased pen, and finding out the truth of "who" you are, in relation to others, is the beginning of a new non-fiction story. There is no other avenue to lasting intimacy.

Questions to Journal:

- What part of Scott and Rita's story evoked emotion in you? Why?

- Do you relate to their struggles to obtain lasting intimacy? If so, how?

- Do you agree that your ability to take care of yourself has a significant influence on your intimacy level with your spouse/lover?

- How does the aging process affect the way you love and how you feel sexually?

- Does your partner's aging affect the depth of your feelings for him or her?

- Do you think blaming is a natural part of most intimate relationships? Is it functional in your relationship?

- Do you have a history of falling in and out of love easily? If so, what is your understanding of this tendency?

- Do you seldom feel you're able to love the total person? If so, how do you understand this tendency?

- Describe the part of your story that maintains irrational beliefs that interfere with your ability to maintain intimacy.

- Are you more comfortable with your spouse or lover when you're alone rather than when you're in public? If so why?

- Do you identify with Gina's story in any way?

- Are you able to set appropriate limits with a lover when you feel he or she is being disrespectful? If not, why?

- Do you understand the pattern you are trying to reestablish in your love relationships to undo childhood hurts?

- Describe the manner in which you received love from each parent. Was it satisfying or dissatisfying to you?

- Describe the manner you saw the parent of the same sex express love.

- Do you find yourself acting similarly in your relationships?

- What role does empathy play in your love relationships?

- Do you think you will ever have lasting love? Explain.

- If you are married or in a committed relationship, do you think you love your partner's essence, his or her character and the core of who they really are?

- Does he or she love the essence of who you really are? If not, can you describe what interferes with a deeper sense of love?

Get Grounded in Experience:

1. Describe your fantasy of the perfect lover/spouse.

2. Record in your journal what this person would bring to your life that is missing. Have a discussion with your lover, spouse or close friend regarding the likelihood of another human being satisfying your longing.

3. Record how much of your longing relates to your attempt to re-write your story without doing the work yourself. In essence, are you looking for a cure through someone else rather than through your own efforts?

Chapter 8:
The More You Love, the More You Get— Community

If you suffer from isolation, you may feel that you have nowhere to turn when you need help. Alternatively, you may feel superior to other groups, races, religions or cultures. When you overcome this sixth challenge, you'll experience less guilt and self-consciousness. You gain an evolving sense of place in the world.

Intimacy that extends to the outside world is the focus of this final challenge. If you seek emotional freedom, you must be involved in the social world. I'm not suggesting that everyone volunteer for the Peace Corps, but that you find a way to connect at whatever level you can. At the very least, that means opening your eyes, mind and heart to information about the inequalities of the world. Personal liberation requires an awareness of the fact that certain societies, cultures and organizations create systems that enslave others.

Many of the world's great spiritual teachers talk about the role of the individual within culture and society. Community is created by individuals, yet uplifts and supports all individuals to new heights collectively. It is a beautiful psychological paradox. The problem is that most of us limit the circle of people we consider our personal community. Social connections provide the platform from which we are able to go out in the world and achieve with balance.

In the Buddhist tradition, one can only ascend to a higher place with a teacher and a *Sangha*, a spiritual community. This community surrounds you, supports you and allows you to ascend to the highest level, Nirvana, through love and understanding.

In the United States, people live the longest in societies that practice connection and what Buddhists call "inter-being." Examples of these communities include Lutherans in the Midwest and Mormons in Utah. The members of these groups live longer than average and psychologists believe part of the reason is that they depend on each other and are raised to care for one another. They empathically engage and let others share their deepest experiences. Connecting through community at the most basic level of life unites us and lets all our spirits rise.

Akin to the stories of spiritual communities, I am going to tell the story of James, a member of one of my most cohesive group coaching programs. He was a hard-driving businessman who suffered from relentless perfectionism that eventually produced a profound depression when his vice president demoted him for his abrasive managing style.

During his time in group, he learned of his terminal illness. He was initially reluctant to talk about his cancer. But before he died in 2007, James shared his fears with the other members. They listened without judgment and supported him without losing themselves in the process. They helped ease his sadness.

When James died, the group shared its pain and loss. One member has said, "I can never come to group on Friday without hearing his voice."

There is no doubt that James benefited from the group process, but the more psychologically interesting aspect is that the group itself is stronger and more intimately connected as a result of having come together for James. We faced the horrible pain and illness of one of our members and emerged as a stronger group of people as a result of our collective strength in the face of tragedy.

The story of James is also surprising because he was not a typical candidate for a group experience. He expected to come for a few weeks and ended up being a veteran member with unusual commitment to the process.

It is cliché now to talk about how it "takes a village to raise a child." This challenge reminds us that every child, every adult, every soul, also helps lift the village.

How Relevant is the Past?

Popular psychology articles frequently talk about the advantage of cognitive behavioral therapy and the new movement of positive psychology versus the old psychoanalytic practice of having people lay on the couch as their past was thoroughly analyzed.

The new psychotherapy movements accent a person's strengths while a person's history is de-emphasized. More traditional analytic therapies believe it is necessary to understand the unconscious meaning of the past in order to free oneself of emotional pain.

James, a cantankerous, yet soft-hearted man, often led the way in our group in terms of deciding how long anyone should spend talking about the past versus doing something different in the present. He didn't always deliver his message with the softest approach. He was "old school" and seldom allowed himself or others to make excuses for their behavior.

He commented in the early days of his group membership that one of the women, Paula, was overweight. This came after she complained of being "tired all the time, never having much energy and feeling self conscious about getting into her bathing suit."

She talked of being chided by her husband about her weight and how her father often teased her about her being chubby as a teen. James was the only group member who risked confronting her weight issues.

She was initially offended, wanted to talk more about her upbringing, but James had had enough and said, "I'm going to stop listening if you don't do anything different. I believe you were criticized as a kid. I don't agree with your husband's tact of chiding you into losing weight either, but I think you'll talk about this for the rest of your life without doing anything to make a change."

Paula grew up with a tremendous focus on her looks, trying one failed diet after another until the point where she just gave up and overate consistently to cope with her nagging doubts about her attractiveness. Her performance addiction manifested itself through her failed attempts to perfect her body.

As a result of her great sensitivity, James's forceful comments caused quite a reaction. Paula accused him of not understanding, of being like her father and basically appealed to the group for support. Person after person spoke and, to her surprise, they agreed with James. They had been reluctant, where he had no reservation to speak his mind.

I was asked at one point what I thought. I pointed out that we had spent considerable time listening to Paula talk about her past. I also agreed with James that Paula had a way of using the past to prevent growth in the present. My position has always been that the past should be explored if it interferes with the present. Once the effects of the past are understood, it is time to take action in a new direction.

Change, as we have discussed, is an active process.

Some people spend too little time on understanding their history; some spend too much time. Some people need to understand the novel they wrote and others will use their biased story as a defense to remain at an impasse in their lives.

We should focus on the past to understand what drives our behavior.

We should not focus retroactively to blame people and hold them accountable for changes we are reluctant or afraid to make ourselves.

Unlikely Friends

James and Paula ironically became close friends and she was more supportive of him than anyone else once he became sick. They forged an honest relationship that was initially based on hurt and ultimately based on respect and the desire to learn.

Paula often returned James' frankness when he would talk of his wife, a wife he was separated from for many years but never divorced. James was our oldest member, in his early seventies, when he was diagnosed with lung cancer. He had been separated from his wife since his late thirties, and claimed to delay divorce because it was simply not necessary.

His rationales were as impressive as Paula's reasons for not exercising and taking better care of herself.

We discovered they had more in common than seemed to meet the eye. They both were very direct with others, both needed to develop more tact with their delivery and neither liked being confronted when their reasoning for their behavior didn't make sense.

Paula was often reminded by James when she began to moan about her weight, "Here you go again. If you didn't exercise this week, I don't want to hear any whining." She would often laugh and call him the one with the longest record for marital separation. "Of course I know you have no feelings for your wife. You haven't fooled me; you love your wife. You're just too stubborn to admit it."

For James, this aspect of the past was never resolved, therefore it would keep coming up whenever he would attempt to become involved with another woman. We asked him many times why his relationships would be so short-lived. He was a handsome, articulate man but seemed to always have one reason or another as to why he would break off a relationship. "They get too serious too soon. I don't want anybody telling me what to do with my time."

Whenever intimacy was discussed, it became apparent that James didn't trust women. Alice, another group member, was his counterpart—divorced and bitter. She and James often tangled as to which sex was the most distrustful. Her ex-husband had an affair with her close friend and later married her. James felt rejected by his wife because she complained of his inability to express feelings and to his frequent tendency to run away when disappointed. Alice and he had preconceived notions of the other gender that were hard to alter. He once called her a "man-hater." She called him "paranoid and afraid of women."

On one occasion I commented to both of them that they had much in common. Of course both made a face at first, but their expressions became quite solemn when I indicated that they shared broken hearts that never healed. I went on to say they shared distrust and fear of the opposite sex, loneliness and a fear of aging alone, a deep love for their children and ethical values, both valuing truth and character more than material possessions.

As time went on, they forged an unlikely connection. Alice left group before James was diagnosed and they parted as friends who had come to respect each other. Alice apologized to James in her last session. "You taught me that women are not the only ones who hurt and most importantly you taught me that some men are honest and trustworthy, men like you."

James had tears in his eyes that day, something we had never seen before. He told Alice that, for so long, he just assumed she didn't like him. "I didn't know how to look beyond the surface and realize you were hurting just as much as me."

Group members still comment today of those infamous interactions between James, Alice and Paula. Their interactions and conflicts, taught us all to expand our empathy, look beyond the cover of the book, understand each person's novel and emerge with new truth, new growth and a revised, more accurate personal story.

Each of them was driven by *the curse* for different reasons; but ultimately, each was driven in a different direction to rewrite the internal stories that had plagued them for years.

Dying Love

Why does one person's terminal illness create strength never imagined among strangers?

Friendship is one of the key factors in longevity. The story of James, this cantankerous, passionate man with high values and a strong sense of responsibility, provides a profound answer.

James was gruff but honest and, as I mentioned, he needed to learn to deliver his points with more sensitivity. His belief system stated that if you're speaking the truth, the delivery doesn't need to be politically correct.

He learned, as did others, that expanding his empathic range made communicating the truth far more acceptable and less offensive to others. People can speak the truth carelessly or compassionately. The latter has far more impact and arouses less suspicion about the sender's objective.

A particular Friday morning is exemplary of this process in motion. James came to group unusually quiet and when asked what was on his mind, he began to tear. He couldn't speak for a few minutes, coughing as he usually did when he was about to reveal something that was particularly difficult for him.

He finally told us, "The cancer is back. This time it's in my liver. They can't do anything else. I think I'm going to die."

He began to cry deeply, sobbing at one point. We were watching the man who'd lived a tough life, had overcome many odds, who never showed much emotion become suddenly vulnerable before our eyes. He was afraid and his emotion evoked emotion in everyone else. In that moment we were witnessing his humanity; his tough exterior had disappeared and he was instantly more likable than ever before.

James didn't get along with all the males in the group. As I said, he could be cantankerous. He had told one member to stop whining and get a divorce and another to stop complaining about his drinking problem and quit. "Just do it."

As time went on, James learned to be more empathic. He began to see the gray in the world and he once indicated that he realized he knew less about people after being in group than when he had started. Several group members commented that they thought this was progress. He was closer to the truth—the truth about life and about himself.

Just as James was becoming more open, he became terminally ill. I remember visiting him in his home in the last days of his life. He looked at me, and while patting his yellow lab, Sam, said, "We weren't doctor/patient. We were friends, and I thank you for being with me all the way."

We Are All More Alike Than We Are Different

It has been said that *we are all more alike than different*. I think this was proven in James's emotional journey in our group. His illness rendered him more emotional, less protective of his sense of self and, as a result, he became more accessible—easier to be close to. In this process, other members were more able to let their guard down as each person's true essence began to emerge.

In the face of mortality, each individual's spirit is enhanced and enlivened. We are closer because we have dealt with the end of life and remained spiritual despite mortality's victory. Communities built on sincerity, honesty and the desire to grow collectively create faith in the positive potential of its members.

I was sitting in a church pew the day of James's funeral when I felt a tap on my shoulder. It was Alice. "I thought I should be here. He taught me so much and I never expected I would feel his loss this way." As the funeral mass proceeded, we saw a woman moving toward the podium to give the eulogy. Alice and I were trying to figure out who this woman was; at the same time we both realized who it was.

James had written a letter to his wife, the wife he had been separated from for many years, asking her to deliver his final farewell. James had learned much in our little group on Friday mornings, but at that moment we both wished he had more time—time to express the love that had been hidden under painful hurts of the past. We wished he had rewritten the story of his marriage with new vision and less fear of being hurt.

We realized a rich opportunity for renewed love had been missed. I think this realization has made each member a bit more immediate in their lives, more likely to explore hurts with others rather than stubbornly retreating into their sadness and pride.

Since that time, many broken hearts have been healed through our group sessions, much resentment clarified and resolved and most importantly, we have all learned over and over again that we are all more alike than different. What a world it would be if this truth were a universal belief.

Every Man Dies, Not Every Man Lives

During the time of James' illness, my Uncle Frank was undergoing the same experience. He also was terminally ill with advanced lung cancer. The last summer of their lives, while I was vacationing in Maine, I would call each of them in succession while I was at the beach and have them listen to the ocean.

They both had many common likes, although they never knew each other. My uncle and James loved the ocean, both knew they would never travel to Cape Cod or Maine again and both enjoyed the sounds of the ocean as the seagulls could be heard in the distance while we talked.

I mention my uncle because he was another profound example of how the ability to relate and form close relationships with others is sustaining, even in the most difficult and painful times.

One of our daughters once asked if it was hard for me to visit my uncle, knowing he was dying and so uncomfortable (his pulmonary illness made it difficult for him to breathe and his oxygen tank was often in use.) I was surprised to realize it was never difficult. We spent very little time talking of his illness. He was high spirited on almost all occasions. I don't mean that he was full of energy, but he was genuinely pleased to see me.

We both had a deep love of family and would talk about our children, his grandchildren, their accomplishments and the funny things they say and do. He would talk of his life, all the crazy moments of the past and most importantly, we would laugh together as he recalled his childhood history and the many twists and unexpected turns he experienced in his lifetime.

He loved food, especially Italian food, so I would go to his favorite market, buy all the foods he liked and even though he couldn't eat much, he enjoyed the process of sitting together with the smells of great food in the air.

As his illness progressed, he and my aunt moved to live with my cousin and his family in an in-law apartment. This new location made it necessary for him to transfer to a rehab center in Rhode Island.

He made so many friends at the new facility. He would tell me stories of each of them, often reading the cards they would send when he would be hospitalized. His physician became so fond of him, he would come to my uncle's in-law apartment for lunch, just to talk and spend enjoyable times with him.

My uncle found common ground with so many of these new people. Initially, the staff at the former rehab thought it might be too difficult for him to transfer his care. I think it actually helped him as he had the opportunity to forge new relationships with new personalities.

When my uncle was first diagnosed, his first pulmonary specialist told him to go to Vegas. "Spend your money and have a good time. There's not much else we can do for you." The doctor gave him six months to live, but two and a half years later, he was still alive. A lesson to all of us—before we eliminate hope, we need to understand the unique personality of the person we are addressing.

I would ask my uncle how he managed to move forward and he would tear up and tell me he wanted to be here "for one more Christmas."

He and James both had a strong spiritual side, each devoting time to spiritual practice weekly. Their beliefs were different, but they both believed in something beyond themselves. Both men were outgoing, not any more confident than the rest of us, but they were people who were going to make connections, to reach out while trying to find the common ground.

My uncle was always a person who was not afraid to relate to others seemingly unlike himself and James was developing this ability. I highlight this tendency as I often wondered how I would be in the same situation. Would I have the courage to enjoy life knowing it was ending, feeling pain in almost every breath?

My uncle not only enjoyed that initial Christmas but the next one as well. He could only sip soup that final holiday, but I could see in his eyes a deep sense of appreciation. He had just returned from his last hospitalization when he told me, "I made it one more time. I told you I was coming home again."

In his heart he had triumphed. He was with those who gave him sustenance and hardly realized that he gave us all the gift of embracing life as never before. At his funeral my cousin Frank III, while delivering his eulogy, said that I was like a second son to my uncle. I felt my heart burst with emotion when I heard those words. I could barely contain myself.

The sadness and joy were simultaneous and overwhelming. I had never received a greater honor.

I relate the story of my uncle as I was often interacting with James during the same time frame.

James was learning to be less judgmental and more open with others, rather than categorizing people quickly and responding as if he knew another without sufficient data. He struggled with people at times, although he was trying hard to be connected. He was grasping a new way of relating and told me he was seeing results with his adult children and other friends in his life. (If only he had lived longer, he could have regained the closeness he once felt with his wife.) He was learning on a weekly basis how to make relationships with people he would have never associated with in the past.

My uncle had these interpersonal skills in his repertoire. You could drop him anywhere in the universe and I truly believe he would make friends. James was evolving to a level of interpersonal empathy that my uncle had experienced most of his life. They both ended life feeling love—one having developed greater range than the other for establishing and maintaining intimacy, but both with the same longings for closeness as the other.

If you are reading this book, you are probably wondering where you fit in terms of the capacity to bring love into your life. My uncle never attained celebrity status in the world, but I am sure he left this life with a feeling of satisfaction we all desire. He was a celebrity in his own community. James left his life knowing he had the courage to move forward. He was making valiant efforts to be a better person, a better communicator.

We are innately programmed for empathy and intimacy. To what degree we move closer to the larger community in our lives is directly correlated to resolving the emotional trials we have discussed. No other effort you make in your life could be as worthwhile.

Questions to Journal:

- How diverse is your circle of friends?

- Are you threatened to establish friends who initially seem unlike yourself? If so why?

- Do you relate or identify with James? Which aspect of his personality is akin to your own?

- Do you relate or identify with Paula? What aspect of her personality is akin to your own?

- Are these attributes that support a positive, personal story or do they detract from your overall well-being?

- Is it a norm in your closest circle of friends to be tactfully honest?

- If not, what is the threat to genuine relating?

- Do you believe that, in the final analysis, human beings are more alike than different?

- What are the reasons for your perspective?

- Can you relate to the personality of my Uncle Frank?

- Do you think you would use your community of friends to help you through a terminal illness?

- If not, what would prevent you from letting others in on your experience?

- Would you be comfortable sharing your emotional pain with your friends, or do you think you would be a burden?

- Do you believe that vulnerability and strength can coexist?

- If not, detail your reasons for thinking these traits are incompatible.

- Do you believe we need to develop compassion beyond our circle of friends and family to people of other backgrounds and races, or do you believe this moving outward is unnecessary for well-being?

- What personal qualities do you think you need to develop further to be able to relate to a diverse group of people in a meaningful way?

Get Grounded in Experience

1. If you aren't already, join a community where you need not participate as a leader but more importantly, as a member and contributor. Try to appreciate the day-to-day experience of being in partnership with others.

2. Make a significant effort to establish a relationship with a member of the group who seems least like you.

4th Stage—Recognize How Your Story Distorts Your Thinking

If you overcome the universal emotional trials, you will have a greater sense of self, defined by your own worth (values) instead of by external markers. You will be more confident, free to move into the future with energy, courage and joy. You will have flexibility, stamina and peace of mind. You'll lose guilt and self-consciousness and you will gain the ability to love others, as well as the capacity to be loved in return.

In this stage we will begin discussing the solutions to these challenges that negatively affect and skew our day to day experience and, of course, the underlying addiction to performance that has amplified its hold on you. Your thinking will reinforce old stories, and it takes a new and empowering story deliberately and consciously created to change ingrained thinking.

I will explain these distortions in thinking that can make matters worse if you are unable to change your point of view. I will also continue to ask you a series of questions that will add to the comprehensive look at your own unique journey toward freedom from *the curse*.

Chapter 9:
Your Best is Good Enough—the Religion of Perfection

Many achievers in our culture have adopted a false belief system that adheres to the theory that if you can perfect your behavior, your appearance and your performance, then all will be well in life.

This is a distortion in thinking that I call the *Religion of Perfection* because, as with all religious upbringings, this notion is a conditioned, unexamined way of seeing the world that was established when we are most impressionable and unfortunately most gullible. I encourage you to learn from all credible sources so as not be imprisoned by the hardwiring of the past, but to examine with today's clarity what is fiction vs. nonfiction.

Our results-oriented, fast-paced society seldom provides the time and patience for healthy development. Young people are often taught that whoever they are in the moment is not enough. It is this dynamic that sows the seeds for this damaging syndrome that is becoming rampant in our society.

We want all people to realize their potential, but when we make achievement intimately associated with perfection (especially at a young age,) we create the blueprint for what ultimately becomes *the curse*. The belief system attached to perfection is the most common and influential distortion in thinking because of its cultural reinforcement.

The practice of this religion comes at all costs and is a primary reason that trading well-being and health for success is so commonplace. How do you stop and take care of yourself when you think you are not good enough? It's difficult to do when you don't think you're worthy.

One of the key questions to ask yourself, to assess your status regarding this new religion is this—*Do you, despite efforts to the contrary, have significant difficulty accepting yourself when you're not at your best?*

Perfection at all costs?

My client Jane, 41-years-old and going through a difficult divorce, was telling me how she was going to compete in a half marathon the coming weekend. She has two young girls, 4 and 7, and holds down a full-time job as an executive in the financial market. She'd just relocated a week before and was stressed because her training for the race was not as good as she had hoped.

"I know what you're going to say Dr. C, 'Just go run, have fun, put the time issue behind me and appreciate the fact that I can compete at all considering the circumstances.' But I just have so much difficultly letting go, letting myself just be less than what I know I can be under ideal circumstances."

As much as she tries, Jane can't quite do what her heart is telling her, which would be a more balanced, healthier way to approach this race; where she might not be at her best, but would perform "well." She has not, as of yet, thoroughly understood her fictional story well enough to actually be able to implement the shift in thinking that would make her more at ease when situations like this don't allow for excellent performance. *She can't yet differentiate between situational variables and personal capability.*

What do I mean?

Sometimes in life, no matter how capable we are situations do not allow us to perform excellently, even if we have the capability. Yes, she could kill herself in this race and beat last year's time, but would the achievement really make her feel better in the long run? No!

Besides running herself down into a depleted state, the success would be fleeting and every subsequent race would have the same unpleasant pressure associated with it. If she understood the fictional story within her and more of the ideas about herself that are just not true, she would be able to take pride in the fact that, given the circumstance, she is already a winner. After all she is able to run thirteen miles, work full-time in a pressured job, while still being able to be a wonderful mom to two young children all while going through a move and a divorce.

"Feeling Never Enough" Starts Early

Jane grew up a chubby girl, but her older sister and younger brother were thin and quite attractive. Her older sister was selected as "best looking" in her senior year of high school, dated a lot and was considered by many to be very pretty and outgoing. Jane, on the other hand, was overweight and not nearly as popular as her sister. They went to high school at the same time—Jane being two years behind—so Jane saw firsthand what appearance can mean in the validation department.

Jane got good grades, did not date until her senior year and, for her last two years of college, stayed with one boyfriend—in fact, he was her only boyfriend. He eventually went on to graduate school and left her for someone else. Jane met her soon-to-be-ex-husband shortly thereafter and was married within eighteen months.

She was secretly thrilled to be the first to marry among her siblings. She was especially thrilled that her older sister would be the bridesmaid and not the bride (showing her performance addiction.) She had always assumed it would be the other way around. Of course her assessment of her husband-to-be was based on *image love* which we will discuss in Chapter 11.

Perfectionism Attracts More Perfection

Jane's fiancé was a "go-getter." He really wanted to make something of himself. She couldn't believe in her heart that she had finally found someone who loved her so much. She even started to exercise the year they met. She was uplifted by the attention she received and began losing weight and liking herself more and more.

She attributed "the new Jane" to her fiancé's love. He gave her the confidence to move into areas that had always been intimidating—exercise, asserting herself, dressing sexier, etc. She was elated to be engaged and planning her wedding was her sole preoccupation for a year. They married and, for a time, it went fairly well. She had difficulty being comfortable sexually but as time went on, she became more at ease.

Unfortunately, she realized her husband steadily lost interest and she interpreted this as due to her lack of attractiveness. After those initial years of marriage, she found her husband to be a driven, preoccupied achiever who seldom had much energy left for being a spouse or father. He excelled in the corporate world and led a fairly isolated life otherwise. The more he achieved in his job, the less he had to give at home.

She was depressed regarding his lack of attention to her during her pregnancies and she feared that the marriage would eventually end. But, in the process, she kept trying to look better, be more sexual and tried more approaches to gain his interest. These attempts worked on occasion but only intermittently. His performance addiction was hidden to her, but now she could see that her obsession with her appearance was equal to his obsession with corporate success at all costs—a common gender split regarding performance addiction.

It Can Change

Ultimately, Jane asked for a divorce and he reluctantly agreed. He offered to change, but she had lost all feelings for him and was resolved to face life alone. She came to group after one of my clients recommended she read *Performance Addiction*. She did and she finally began to understand what was going on in her life that made her feel cursed.

Today, she has begun the process of understanding her mythical belief in perfection, but it is a cognitive understanding and not yet an emotional change. It will take time and practice to ultimately become free of the underpinning story she has yet to uncover and rewrite. Hopefully, when she runs the race, some of these insights will kick in, but as I cautioned her, she needs to develop tolerance, for this process is not a sprint... but a full marathon.

As Jane continues her self-work, she will realize that healthy, high-achieving people, including many exceptional athletes, do not approach performance in an addicted way. They have tolerance of their ability to perform based on present circumstance and they set expectations accordingly. They perform exceedingly well on a relatively consistent basis because they maintain balance and well-being.

As Jane continues on this emotional journey, it will be absolutely critical that she can differentiate between situational stressors that compromise her abilities (like her move and divorce,) versus those times when the outcomes in her life are truly due to her lack of capability. Most people suffering from any aspect of *the curse* seldom make this distinction.

How do you change the hardwiring, the deep conditioning that says if you don't act or appear perfect, you will lose the esteem of others?

Changing the Hardwiring of Perfection

In one of my recent group sessions, a new member asked if others tell their bosses, coworkers or friends that they come to group. He was anxious that this could hurt his performance review at work and also said he felt ashamed that he couldn't balance his life on his own. He said he hadn't even told his closest friends.

One of our oldest members, also a fellow engineer at a prestigious company, admitted, "I was very embarrassed at first. My anxiety over performance had gotten so bad, I thought I was having a heart attack and ended up in the emergency room."

"Over time I have learned that the people I want in my life understand and those that don't, I find myself caring much less about. It has been sort of a test for me to know who to trust and also to find out who 'gets it' (Healthy High Achievers.) Trust me, I was one of those guys who didn't 'get it' at first."

Our newest member can't internalize this new view, but he will in time. He will because he'll learn from some of the most capable people he will ever encounter. He will learn we are leading a fraudulent life when we mask vulnerability, but we are leading a life of wisdom when we acknowledge that we will never perfect ourselves, because the human race is by its very nature imperfect.

We gain comfort when we develop an understanding of this fact and live our lives with this awareness embedded in our hearts. I am not encouraging anyone to advertise vulnerability in situations where it will clearly hurt you. Obviously, disclosing to colleagues and superiors is a very sensitive issue and one must proceed cautiously. On the other hand, if you suffer from the *religion of perfection*, I know you have exaggerated the consequences of not being perfect. Our newest member can't let go of this notion without fear, but we all need to test the waters and see if "less than perfect" really has the effects on others we imagine.

Remember it's certain aspects of your novel that created this distortion; and a novel is fiction. We are creating a new story at this point, a non-fiction book about your life that will be far more reliable in predicting behavior than the biased story of the past; when new, more empowering aspects of your story are in place the hardwiring around perfectionist thinking changes.

Feeling like a Fraud

Our newest member felt the pressure of perfectionism to a debilitating degree, so much so that he ended up thinking he was a fraud because he couldn't balance his life. Little did he know that he now belongs to an extremely exclusive group of capable people, who have had the same difficulty.

Ironically, he was given a promotion two weeks prior to joining the group, giving him the responsibility of managing a Northeast territory that is only managed by very high achievers. Nevertheless, he feels like he's "faking it" and will be found out—despite his stellar professional track record.

What is fraudulent is the cover up in his thinking that is taking its toll on his well-being and the ability to live in balance. If he could come to see the strength in self-disclosure and be honest about his experiences, he would realize that he is not alone.

Group interactions, in particular, increase our objectivity about ourselves and lessen the pressure and extreme expectations we have of ourselves. As our new member expresses what seems true for him in his new role, his hardwiring will likely change.

The other night one of the men in my group session stated that the group is the only place he truly talks about his vulnerabilities. He went on to say he would be petrified for his friends to know his struggles: high blood pressure, shame about the fact that he never finished college and regret regarding his self-centered behavior in his last marriage.

Mary, a veteran member, told him, "Everything you hide from your friends, you hide from yourself. Trust me; I didn't know for years I was duping myself."

The sense of being a fraud comes then from our own self-deception. We expend energy, masking our vulnerabilities to others while not realizing the same process is occurring internally. We think that by not exposing ourselves, we're protecting ourselves but, in fact, we are depleting our energy and missing the chance to gain from the closeness that genuine relating brings.

This is a dangerous process indeed because we become fraudulent in our own internal world, which results in lack of self-awareness and a constant drain on our self-worth. Belief in self cannot be maintained by pretense; this dynamic consumes energy and brings no return in investment.

Get Grounded in the Experience

We need new experiences to change our old view of ourselves. As we receive new feedback from people who are rational and objective, we have the opportunity to form more accurate views of behaviors that have been biased because of *the curse*.

For instance, as my patient ventures out into his social world, he may experiment with sharing his imperfections with others at appropriate times. He may find out, as he has in the group, that good people are seldom as judgmental as he imagines.

As I have indicated earlier, change is an active process. It takes courage to take the risk to behave differently, and when we do, we are in the process of rewriting the past with new information.

I have a client who recently joined a dating service after going through a painful divorce. Mike was an exceptional college athlete and excelled academically, but the fact that he attended a state school is as embarrassing to him as the blue collar town in which he grew up. He works in the financial markets with many high-powered men and woman, and several of his associates have graduated from Ivy League schools.

Mike was initially intimidated by some of his fellow group members as their credentials seemed to exceed his. We worked with him in group regarding his shame, his family's poverty and not attending a prestigious college. We helped him lessen his preoccupation with his baldness, and as a result, I think we realistically changed his fixed view of men in their forties without hair.

The irony is that I know the women in the group find him quite attractive and particularly like the commitment he has made to become a better listener. Mike is a man who has always felt "less than," and as a result, has had trouble relaxing into conversations without interrupting as a result of his anxiety.

One of his first encounters with the dating service was an arranged dinner where he met two female physicians and one college professor. "I was so anxious when they sat me next to the dermatologist, my heart started to beat so fast I could hear it. Then after a few minutes, the group's comments clicked in: 'listen more than you talk, slow down and try to really get to know the other person without trying to impress.' I held my tongue, asked more questions than talking about myself. I found her life so interesting—her interest in yoga, spirituality and travel.

As the night went on, I could see we were making a connection. After dinner we walked down the driveway together. She stopped at one point, looked at me rather shyly and asked me if I would call her. I immediately asked 'why' and then realized I probably blew it, showing my inadequacy rather then just accepting her interest.

But to my surprise, she gently answered the question, 'You're the only man here who knows how to listen and you seem genuinely interested in me not just because I'm a doctor. Besides that, you have a great smile.' I guess I have the group to thank for that!"

Mike's new experience taught him something he had missed most of his adult life: *trying to impress is not impressive.*

Knowing how to engage another person, not perfectly but realistically and authentically, is amazingly appealing to most people. Mike had tried so hard for so long to eliminate his imperfections and improve himself, that he had lost his very essence.

Underneath his anxiety is a humble person who truly likes being with people. When he relaxes, Mike is fun to interact with, contrary to his previous beliefs. The skills he is allowing to blossom are far more related to success than curly hair and an impressive resume.

Even Media is Delivering a New Experience

It is interesting to me that in our current societal downturn (economic woes, international worry, terrorist threats, etc.,) the fastest growing TV phenomena—the reality show—is almost exclusively focused on humiliating failure.

Shows like "Wipeout" have been called "the salve for American depression." Failure on these shows is akin to success. Is this trend providing relief for Americans who are burnt out on performance?

Are the reality shows identifying a need in our society, showing us how to put the brakes on and stop the relentless pressure to perfect ourselves? Are they allowing, for a brief moment, the sanction to come up seemingly short and be okay with it? To try our best but to find humanness in outcomes no matter what they are?

In the case of "Wipeout," the courses the contestants are competing in are very challenging and coming up short is not the intention, but it happens. Sometimes our best efforts fail for no fault of our own; there are other circumstances at play. It appears that many people are enjoying watching reality show episodes combining humor and failure. An odd combination to most achievers!

Freedom Comes with Imperfection

It is so liberating when we trust ourselves enough to be ourselves. As we give up the need and obsession to perfect ourselves (particularly in the presence of others who care), we often realize that the road to intimacy and internal calm comes when we open our humanness to the world, rather than continuing all our fruitless efforts to win others over through pretending to be more than who we really are.

A learning that is hard to digest for achievers is the truism that allowing our imperfect selves to be revealed makes us more appealing and more connected to the human frailties that exist in all of us.

We relax other people and ourselves when we give up the pretense, because it takes so much work to always be on guard, to be so concerned with perfecting our speech and behavior. Perfectionism hinders our creativity and our ability to see the world more comprehensively, and of course, it makes us self-absorbed which means we miss the opportunity to be present, engage and learn from others.

We all need to try our best to reach our potential, but the highest level of achievement is always accompanied with balance. Achievement within the structure of a balanced life is not only a wonderful, subjective feeling, but it is also an incredibly attractive model for others, especially in our current "performance at all costs" culture.

Questions to Journal:

- Are you confusing the circumstances that limit your ability to perform with a lack of capability?

- Do you find it threatening to let go of the notion that people will only be impressed with you if you are at the top of your game?

- Does everything in your life have to be done to your level of perfection which is often higher than anyone else's? If so, how come?

- Do you think there is no sense in trying to do something unless you can do it perfectly? (ex. "I don't attempt things that I can't do well.")

- Must you always strive to reach the ideal in everything you do because it is in the achievement of the ideal that gives meaning to your life? Explain.

- Do you refrain from disclosing to anyone what goals you're working on, reasoning that way they won't consider you a failure if you don't reach them?

- What's the story in your mind about why you need to be perfect at all costs, even if it means living out of balance and unhealthily?

Get Grounded in Experience

1. This week, try to build tolerance for performing imperfectly, and forge an appropriate philosophy to substantiate why it's the best you can do given the circumstances.

2. Notice what it feels like to do your best, considering current variables, while being satisfied with the outcome.

Chapter 10:
Relax - You Don't Have to Have All the Answers— Pathological Certainty

Are you always certain, feeling like you always need to have the answer? If so, you are exhibiting a classic achiever attribute. This approach can be a major burden with significant negative consequences. Most importantly, it interferes with having a genuine relationship with other people. It is an immediate turn off to be listening to someone who thinks or acts as if he has all the answers.

The central question of this chapter is; "Why do you have the need to give answers at every turn, to appear certain when you are not?"

Pathological certainty, the feeling that you always have to have an answer, is the next distortion in thinking. Of course some people actually believe, through their arrogance, that they are always right. It goes hand-in-hand with perfectionism and most often stems from a fragile sense of self. At the end of the day, it is a cover-up and it prevents you from being free and to think and live better.

The Big Cover-Up

What better way to feel like you've got it all together than to act like it by projecting certainty?

In uncertain times, having all the answers, for at least a little while, gives the illusion that you are problem-free and can handle anything, often in isolation. It will also make you seem like the dependable, go-to person. Ironically, this dynamic is part of *the curse*.

It is an attempt to please those around you by striving for perfection. It leads to feeling defeated, depleted of energy and misunderstood by others who learn to expect that you will perform for them at all costs. It's all a set-up and you are the leading architect through no fault of your own. Pathological certainty is a common way of coping with low self worth.

When you are not in genuine relationships with others and you have your "game face" on, you project an image to cover up how you are really feeling inside, which is not peaceful or allowing for vulnerability. Like any other cover-up, you mask your vulnerability. What better way to achieve your goal than to dominate the conversation and have all the answers?

Unfortunately, the show of certainty you put on (most often an image of wealth and wisdom which may be authentic at times but often isn't,) can leave you dealing with expectations you've set that you have to live up to with others.

It's a Form of Perfection

You are still a follower of the *"religion of perfection"* if you feel like you always have to have the right answers. Born of many of the same causes as perfectionism, it's a very black and white way of looking at the world. When you have perfectionist thinking, chances are very good your psychology lends itself to *pathological certainty.*

Inferiority and superiority complexes tend to develop into a life of pathological certainty. The inferior often wants to appear more certain than they are and the superior is often acting in line with how they think they are. Both of these complexes are coping mechanisms for an unresolved past, an addiction to performance and the consequent emotional trials.

For example, past humiliations or the idealization of a parent who exhibited pathological certainty can lead to unwillingness to accept a point of view other than your own. Some pass this off as expediency, not wanting to waste time by allowing input from others. After all, that would require genuine relating and that's not exactly the top skill of a performance addict or a sufferer of *the curse*.

A likely reality is that you do not want rejection or the emotional "hit" that the rejection would create. It may also mean admitting, "No, I don't have it all together" and that may seem outside the character of your distorted sense of self—all that you have wrapped up in your story; thus, not being certain about the answer opens up a sort of emotional "no man's land" and "inbetween-ness" that is very uncomfortable. Certainty can be like a drug, and for an addict who has limited skills in coping with uncertainty, this can be very disconcerting.

Your Sense of Self

When an achiever has a fragile sense of self, it's likely they are going to want to cover up and "be strong," "live strong," etc., and project confidence and assuredness.

But what's the alternative? Wear how you really feel on your sleeve, in public? *As a result, the public and private "you" become more and more separate.* The difference between your game face, your social face, and how you really are, becomes more disparate.

With a strong sense of self, you don't have to be preoccupied with maintaining an image. You have faith that if there is a "right answer" you will reach that conclusion because you're surrounded by intelligent people. You're in partnership with colleagues, friends and family. You will have the wisdom to know that, at times, there is no "right answer" and when certainty can be attained it is often reached by consensus.

Even if you truly know the answer without consultation, a strong sense of self allows you to listen to other points of view regardless, always realizing that positive partnerships are made through discussion and respect. If you have internal strength, you can wait, listen and then give your opinion.

In some of our group discussions, achievers are often so eager to speak that some actually raise their hands and look to me for the microphone. They can't wait to establish their worth in the presence of others.

Ironically, that kind of impulsive behavior does not win them points with their fellow members.

Separating Yourself

Pathological certainty is a way of separating yourself from people—the opposite of what your goal may be. You may love people and desire intimate relationships. Yet afflicted by *the curse*, your attempt to create a better story is not working, as it is not grounded in truth (this is likely also felt by others.)

Attempting to be certain is never going to solve what is missing or hurting inside you. It ultimately puts you in a vulnerable position and distances you from others who have problems with your rigidity, as you will see in the following example.

It's Either Black or White

Not long ago my wife and I were having dinner with a group of friends we have known for years and love very much. We are all from different walks of life but have come together over time for various reasons.

One of my friend's oldest daughters is attending a private, Catholic school in the area and she was assigned a paper on comparing two religions to Catholicism. She came home while we were having dinner and asked if she could talk to me for a few minutes about the paper before we left that evening. I inquired about her interest and my friend Liam said, "Anne thinks you'll know something about Buddhism. I hope you're not going to warp her young mind."

Everyone chuckled a bit, but it was a tense moment, as we all knew how Liam felt about religion. He was raised in a large Irish-Catholic family and faith has been a pivotal force in his parents' and siblings' lives. His family and all its members are the type of people you feel instantly comfortable with—very outgoing, warm, incredibly funny and unusually generous. They have suffered through many tragedies since I have known them and their beliefs have helped them immensely. They have weathered several storms, including the death of their father and a car accident that took their youngest sister's life.

So, given this background, you can imagine why Liam feels so doggedly about being Catholic. As the evening ensued, we began to talk more about religion. Liam's wife asked me a few questions about Buddhism, and to my surprise she seemed quite interested in the philosophy of living that is unique to Tibetan Buddhists.

I could see Liam was not feeling comfortable with this conversation, especially as his daughter sat at the table listening eagerly. "Arthur, sometimes you really amaze me, all that education and you can get influenced so easily. You sound like you're becoming a Buddhist."

I replied that I didn't understand why he felt so strongly, we were only talking. He went on to say that the church has been a lifesaver for him and that his belief in Jesus Christ has given him the strength to overcome so many bad times. He related how he feels so peaceful in church on Sunday and how he knew I was raised the same way.

I commented that I could understand his feelings and perspective, but if he had been born in Tibet, he might be saying the same thing about Buddhism. The group at the table was obviously feeling a bit uncomfortable. After all, we were supposed to be having dinner and just hanging out on a Saturday night.

Fortunately or unfortunately, one last question from Liam's daughter caused the fire to be re-ignited. She asked me if I knew of any comparisons between Buddha and Jesus. I commented that there are many texts that state it was likely that Jesus was influenced by Buddha. I then recommended two books by Thich Nhat Hanh, *Living Buddha, Living Christ* and *Going Home: Jesus and Buddha as Brothers*.

Well, this was just too much for Liam and he emphatically told Sara she should not read those books. There is one Son of God and it is certainly not Buddha.

One of my tactful friends changed the subject that night, but I will always remember the dialogue. Why? Because Liam is a good man with good character, but he is also what many call a "black and white" thinker. Yes, he is a high achiever, although I do not think he sees himself as such.

He does not fret on the big issues such as: Should we be in Iraq? Should we allow gay marriage? The answer is "yes" to Iraq and "no" to gay marriage. It's not something he debates in his mind. He follows the President and he follows the church. He has his map and that's that.

You might ask how we became friends. Well, his wife Anne is a psychiatric nurse I worked with for years. When she re-married several years ago, I met Liam. Anne is a wonderful person and overly giving, but is extremely indecisive. You can understand the attraction.

Liam is the salve for Anne's doubt in life. Liam is a very physical man, as I am, so we found common ground in working out together, running on the beach and, in certain ways, I think he is fascinated by my life as it seems so bizarre to him. He once asked me how I could stand listening to people "complain" all day. "I could never do it. I like a clear outcome with none of this psycho babble for excusing people for not taking responsibility for their life."

Tough love is not exactly what Liam means, as I have seen him melt in interactions with his daughter, but I think his image of being the "go-to guy" is extremely important to his identity. He loves the Nike ad, "Just Do It." Problem is, not all of us can "Just do it" if we were not given the right tools to utilize. Liam, for instance, was never helped in developing the faith in himself that would allow him to cope with diversity with ease rather than with threat.

Two Approaches to the Answer

Interestingly, I started using the term *pathological certainty* when I was a young intern being supervised by a respected psychoanalyst. A number of us would present our cases to him in supervision and he would, after hearing about the patient for less than 20 minutes, make a diagnosis.

He was famous for saying, "Now all you have to do is sit in the chair for a few years and interpret his OCD or her neurosis."

I made the mistake one day of asking him how he could be so certain of the diagnosis of a person he'd never met, after only listening to a history of an individual for less than a half hour. His answer was, "When you have been doing this work as long as I have, it doesn't take forever to figure out that *certain* symptoms lead to a *certain* diagnosis."

I will always remember the emphasis on the word "certain." I think I learned more from him that year on what *not to do*, rather than which way to proceed with a patient.

Ironically, another psychoanalyst supervised me the second half of that same year and his approach to the world was entirely different. He was one of the best teachers I've ever had. He made decisions decisively, but only after taking time to ascertain the facts. He was unusually comfortable with not having an immediate answer.

I realized that year the difference in the two men. My second supervisor had suffered in his personal life and emerged whole. He grew up with a mentally-challenged sister and developed unusual empathy for the less fortunate in life. He clearly was a person who had faith in himself but also felt, and I emphasize *felt*, the vulnerability that could be bestowed on any of us at any time.

He also was very identified with his Jewish identity, had been to Israel several times, and yet didn't seem to have any hatred for Arabs or for the Palestinians. He was a student of the Holocaust and I have no doubt that these experiences opened him up to the imperfections of human beings. He had a way of coaxing the better parts of people to the surface. I think this happened because clients could sense he understood in his heart, not just in his head.

A Way of Being

Pathological certainty is a dangerous way of being from many perspectives. Of course, it cuts off connecting to people that are different from us. Most of us have had the unfortunate experience of seeing a physician who gives an answer when they really don't have one.

On the other hand, we have experienced a physician who will say, "I'm not sure. Why don't I refer you to Dr. Jones; he specializes in this type of problem." Or he says he will do some research, talk to colleagues and get back to you.

With whom do you feel more comfortable? Do you like the quick answer, the answer that provides an immediate outcome or can you tolerate a realistic wait if it will provide a more accurate diagnosis?

Are You a Confabulator?

To confabulate means to construct false answers to a question while genuinely believing that you are telling the truth. William Hirstein, author of the book, Brain Fiction, reflects on "knowledge deficits." Confabulators suffer from a derailment of processes by which we ascertain our beliefs about the world. Their brains produce fast and loose hypotheses, but crucially, fail to check them for accuracy.

Instead, confabulators experience a "pathological certainty" that whatever springs to mind is simply true, despite potentially overwhelming evidence to the contrary. Their inability to crosscheck their beliefs blocks them from acknowledging how deeply flawed their claims are. Accordingly, they can't perceive or even conceive their own deficits.

One of the most interesting points about confabulation and knowledge is the author's contention that the construction of effective representations by the human brain takes place in degrees.

He then discusses an appropriate consequence of this assertion, which he calls the "degraded representation principle." This principle asserts that if the capacity to represent events of a certain type is diminished in a particular individual, then the likelihood for this individual to confabulate about these events increases.

Of course, some individuals, with limited conscience, confabulate purposely. We all have had the experience of salespeople talking quite convincingly about a product we later determine they know little about. They have a goal—to sell us something. In personal life, the goal is often to impress so that a person's doubts about themselves will be lessened by maintaining the interest of other people.

Depleted Energy and Pathological Certainty

For reasons mentioned earlier, lack of energy leads to expediency and a lack of emotional fortitude to get a stronger sense or broader view of the truth. If your sense of self is fragile and defined by a fixed view of the world, you won't have the emotional fortitude to consider other options.

A punitive self-voice with accompanying low self-worth depletes energy constantly. I consistently witness, as clients begin to feel better about themselves, and can tolerate more uncertainty without loss of esteem, that their energy increases. They are more likely to be more open to diversity. They are far less in need of seemingly being the one in the know.

The Consequences of Certainty

Pathological certainty is a defense. The problem in Liam's case is that he was unaware of his defense, as he felt too threatened to explore his rigidity. If he opened his heart he actually would feel more secure. I know this for a fact as I have seen him slowly become more open as his girls become older. He has been forced to consider other options for their benefit, and I know the love of children often motivates parents to move beyond their comfort zone. I have had this experience many times as our daughters introduced new ideas, new people and new philosophies into our lives.

"Certainty" can have a drug-like effect as one obtains validation for being "so knowledgeable" that it becomes an addictive cycle that is reinforced and, in some instances, it actually works for a time to shore up self-worth. This dynamic is particularly prevalent when the "all knowing one" attracts the overly doubtful person. Each person starts to thrive on the other's role. I have often worked with individuals who have little confidence and are easily taken in by those who project an unusual degree of certainty in their approach to life.

A Difficult Pattern to Break

This is a difficult pattern to break, especially if the individual who projects certainty is actually someone who works hard to obtain data to impress others. We see this dynamic currently as people will act like they know exactly why our economy is suffering or what we need to do to eradicate ourselves from Iraq, without it being a campaign that had merit.

Politicians continually bombard us with simplistic answers and many of us are influenced by their presentation, even though the assertions are not backed up with objective truths. We could say the same for the diet industry, the self-help industry and on and on. So many people who have little faith in their ability to make their way in the world are vulnerable to those who are drenched in certainty.

Pathological Certainty is a Search for Identity

When the sense of self is fragile, we fall prey to those who promise to show us the way. We make them part of our identity and we feel secure for a time. Of course this is short-lived, as we cannot maintain a positive view of ourselves for long if we are blindly following a path we have not created through our own hard work.

We can learn from those who seem to have clear answers as to how we should live, eat, exercise and handle our emotional lives. But if you don't recognize that you are swallowing theory whole because you doubt your ability to think and live in your own unique way, you will find yourself lifted up by the next guru and dropped in short order down the road when you realize that what you were certain about is not the final answer, or certainly not an answer specifically designed for you.

Certainty is not pathological in and of itself. We can't rely on direct experience before we make every decision. However, collaboration with others and using empathy to know who to use as a consultant, makes an enormous difference. This means being open to learning.

Pathological certainty stands in the way of understanding that learning is a life-long process that makes us happy and makes our world forever interesting and meaningful. Continuous learning is a builder of identity. Yet, those who aren't open to new points of view or admitting what they don't know, limit the opportunity to bolster and enhance identity.

You can learn the necessary skills for extraordinary relating and learning if you acknowledge your problems and your shortcomings, and then find others who are further along in the journey to help you. Pretending to know, or acquiring information solely to impress, will wear thin with people over time. It will only bring you more disappointment rather than the quality of intimacy and acceptance you desire.

Questions to Journal:

- Do you secretly wish you would be the one who has the answers to life's problems? Do you feel insecure if you don't know the facts when you're being asked for information? Explain.

- Are you afraid to enter the gray zone in life because you might be perceived as weak and ineffective?

- Do you have the confidence to pursue answers without giving a quick reply to maintain your image?

- Do you respect people who are very decisive as much as those prone to seeing both sides of an issue?

- Are you easily impressed by those who sound confident and all-knowing without closely examining the facts of what they are saying? Are you a good target for the marketers of the world? Why?

Get Grounded in Experience

1. Even if you think you have the answer in a given situation, ask questions of others and try to learn from their perspective. Make a commitment to learn all you can from those around you. Try not to prejudge their ability to contribute.

2. Form a consensus around the answer and see how taking that tact affects your rapport with others.

Chapter 11:
How Your Long-ings Pick Who You Love—Image Love

In recent years, several studies have shown that people who have satisfying relationships, particularly those who are successfully married, are healthier, more balanced and achieve at higher levels than those who are single.

These studies are very telling. While there are a myriad of factors that contribute to these outcomes, the most notable is likely the ability to be in genuine, intimate relationships. **Intimate relationships are the central aspect that helps solve the painful dynamics of *the curse*.** The reality checks provided by close relationships are worth their weight in gold. This feedback loop with those close to us is how we develop emotional stability and become free of distorted thinking—like image love.

As I indicated in the beginning chapters, people with PA or others who are particularly driven to achieve, often have difficulty establishing and maintaining intimate relationships. I am not exclusively referring to romantic love, but also friendships of depth and quality.

Those who are driven to achieve, to the exclusion of close connections with others, are covering up the problems of early development. Achievement then becomes their substitute relationship where control can be had, power can be realized and intimacy is not a requirement.

Hence, *the curse*; they don't have to face their vulnerabilities the way people do willingly and perhaps passionately who have learned how to maintain intimacy. However, once they realize the power of their unresolved past on their present-day behavior, they can begin to change their story and lift the cover that has provided false protection for so many years.

Achievers cover up when vulnerabilities and the emotional challenges they produce are seen as a negative, potentially revealing some part of themselves they feel they cannot face or don't want to reveal. I have had hundreds of conversations with high achieving people who wish they "had a life." In truth they do, at least outwardly and in the eyes of others. Although it is not rich in the intimacy they long for. As a result, they don't feel fulfilled

Love… a Distraction?

Love is a distraction for many achievers because of issues related to control. Even though control is often an illusion, many achievers feel they have less control or loss of control when it comes to intimate relationships.

Is this feeling based on truth? No, they never really had the influence they imagined unless it occurred in a very dysfunctional relationship where their partner didn't feel free to disagree or be autonomous. The loss of control often comes from no longer feeling perfect or confident about their lives as they face vulnerabilities in an intimate relationship.

Hence the distortion in thinking about love is born. In other words, when the story a person tells about himself/herself is proven inaccurate, a true loss of control is experienced. After all, his/her story itself has been a form of control and when that story is not based on the realities that intimacy reveals, it is by default a fictional story. It is inaccurate, and it can cause a whirlwind of difficulties to maintain.

Caught Up to Cover-Up

People who are not in an intimate relationship and are unyieldingly caught up in constant achievement are engaged in a bold attempt to secure love and respect from afar, making love a distraction. As much as they may want love, those who feel *cursed* adopt stories that eliminate the possibility.

It's the classic achiever story of the person who puts the rest of life on hold in order to excel in various ventures—be it a job, a new business, perfecting appearance or various attempts to obtain fame and status.

This is not to say there aren't times when a loving relationship would, in fact, be a distraction. When Tiger Woods was first making his mark and finding his stroke in the PGA, his father Earl worked very hard to help him stay focused. It was a time in his life when he was dedicated toward reaching his goal. This kind of single-minded focus was appropriate for him and his needs at that juncture in his life.

Before long, the impulse for intimacy in a loving relationship beyond that of friends, family and associates, will emerge as a natural human need for all people. Ironically, when Tiger was first engaged, reporters criticized him for not being as focused as in previous years. They questioned his desire to continue to be at the top of the PGA.

Of course, we all know his marriage only solidified his abilities. He continued to excel as always. His marriage allowed him to establish balance in his life. He speaks as much these days about continuing to build his learning foundation for children as he does about golf.

How Your Longings Pick Who You Love

None of us initially falls in love with another person; we fall in love with an image that seems to fulfill our longings, those strong and persistent yearnings or desires that cannot be fulfilled without emotional challenges. No one wants to feel challenged in aspects of our lives where others seem to engage with relative ease.

In the obsession and compulsion of romantic passion, we escape from time, responsibilities and, ultimately, we escape from whatever we are troubled by at the present time. Suddenly, we have found an anti-depressant that works better than any pharmaceutical in overcoming energy depletion or our thoughts about ourselves and our past life, especially in the short term. In the beginning, the object of our affections is often not a real person, our new partner is an object of escape and ecstasy—an object that can take us on a wonderful vacation from ourselves temporarily.

The emotional part of the brain has a powerful influence on relationships. The characteristics that attract you to a person are most likely already determined in your brain's emotional center. If you have PA, it is almost certain that you are looking for an image in another person to uplift your own. This attitude interferes with developing long-term intimacy, seriously compromises your sexual relationship and can only lead to ongoing frustration. You are not engaged in a union based on mutual knowing of each other, but rather a relationship that is being established mainly for functional value. The function is to lift your self-esteem.

Love through the Ages

Image Love manifests differently at various ages, according to gender and marital status. Let me give you a few examples of how some of my clients, at various ages, let their longings govern their love interest to their detriment and one example of how a destructive longing turned into a healthy desire for love of a deeper nature.

Patti is 32, unmarried and recently called me on her cell phone as she was driving with her new boyfriend. She has a terrible history with men, consistently choosing the "biker type" and getting hurt when their character turns out to be less stellar than she had wished. She was reeling with excitement as she called, "Doc, I am in the car with my new boyfriend, the DOCTOR. Did you hear me? The DOCTOR." *(Always remember the image you will project onto another will be directly correlated to your longing at the moment.)*

Patti is a woman who hasn't dated in a few years. She has struggled with ADHD, depression and periodic cocaine abuse. Today she is clean, exercising daily, has lost 22 pounds in the last year and is finally feeling better about herself.

She has said, from the time I met her 18 months ago, that she would not date again until she had pulled her life together, always fearing she would make the same old "stupid" decisions of the past with men. She has characteristically been attracted to men who were impulsive, drug users and people who were not known for stability, but for "the exciting life."

Now, after finishing her academic program, she is working in her first hospital job as an x-ray technician. She met a doctor, a *real* doctor, and she was so excited she could barely control herself.

When she came for her session shortly after the phone call, she asked what I thought after she had told me about her excitement regarding the first doctor she had ever dated. I said, "Patti, it sounds like addictive behavior. You're idealizing this man and you seem to know very little about him."

Needless to say, several weeks later the balloon burst and Patti came to realize that the doctor had many problems of his own—one in particular turned out to be dressing in women's underwear. She noticed, after he slept in her apartment a few times, that her underwear was disappearing. One night sleeping at his place, she stumbled onto her underwear on top of his dryer.

The rest of the story is fairly predictable. Patti was longing for stability in a man, finally wanting to break the patterns of the past and move into a relationship of consistency and normalcy. The doctor was not that person, despite his impressive resume. But she assumed that someone with such credentials must be emotionally stable.

I asked her at one point if she would have dated the doctor if he had been the director of sanitation for her home town, and, of course, she said no. "He isn't even good looking. He was terrible in bed and was completely self-centered. But the worst part is I probably would have stayed with him. For once in my life, my parents were impressed with someone I was dating. My mother told all her friends about the 'doctor' and I finally felt like she was proud of me."

Patti is the younger of two children. Her older brother went to college and is married with children. Patti describes herself as the "eternal aunt," never expecting to be the "mother." Patti's longing at age 32 is to be married to a man unlike the unstable men of the past and to be a mother "before it's too late."

Her deepest longing is to finally impress a mother who is quite taken with the "image" of a person. These longings manifest differently at different ages and with different personality makeup. For instance, my young patient, Mathew, living in an atmosphere of stoic practicality, has a wish of another fashion.

I Just Want to Have Fun!

Mathew is 17 years old, an exceptional athlete and is a very serious young man who seldom laughs. He comes from a pressured background. His dad is an attorney and his mom a financial analyst. Upon meeting the family, I was struck by how rigid everyone seemed.

The dad hardly smiled at all and the mother kept interrupting her son while he tried to explain his recent problems with anxiety and drinking. The first time I saw Mathew exhibit any excitement was one evening when he came in and began telling me about his new girlfriend. "She is so good looking and loves to drink and party. I know she is going places. She just doesn't apply herself. I love going to her house. Her mom even lets us have a few beers. Please don't ever tell my parents. They would kill me."

In a subsequent session, Mathew told me he had sex for the first time with his new love. They drank some beers and made "love" in the basement of her mother's home.

Mathew then went through a period where his grades dropped, his scores on his SAT's were quite poor and his parents and he were in a big struggle.

Mathew is being recruited by Division I schools and is certain to get scholarships.

The issue at hand is his longing. His desire is not unusual for adolescent, high achievers; he wants to have fun. Trust me, I met his parents and they are not fun. I would not feel comfortable with either of them socially. They are the type of people who would be name-dropping all night and would have you in a corner telling you about their stock portfolio until you fell asleep.

Mathew has been pushed to excel since early on in his life. He is now sought after by many coaches throughout the country. Will he actually make it to college? Not if this longing is not realized in a more balanced way than his current method.

Mathew is another example of how our life course can change at any age if we are not aware of the essential emotional nutrients that have been missing in our lives. Mathew is running from the inaccurate story created in his family: namely, that one cannot achieve and have happiness simultaneously. It is my job to help him recognize this inaccuracy as I help him create a more balanced way of achieving. This will only come through experimenting with a new way of being.

Mathew is in a different phase of life than Patti, but both are mis-directed in their search for what has eluded them. They have been unaware of the origin of their quest, so their ability to see clearly is blocked. As a result, they can lose the opportunity to reach their goals in a balanced way.

I Just Want Brad Pitt with Money!

Marilyn is 55 years old, unusually attractive, has a very warm personality and is extremely outgoing. She is the kind of person who makes everyone comfortable, or at least will die trying to do so. She has been in sales her entire adult life and has been quite successful.

She recently ended a long-term marriage in a very contentious court battle. Her husband earned less than her throughout their marriage, owned a business that hardly ever made money but allowed him to golf frequently and hang out at their kids sporting events. Marilyn, however, was expected to bring in the majority of the cash.

They lost their first home due to his ill-advised business deals and unbeknownst to her, owing the IRS mounds of money. She caught him having affairs on three different occasions, but always bought his next excuse for fear of being alone. She also was not confident about raising their kids without him. She began drinking at night to numb the pain and deny the reality of her marriage.

Today, she is divorced, worried she is too old to find anyone who would be interested in her and recently was forced to foreclose on the home she'd bought after the divorce. As business in the economy went south, so did her ability to make mortgage payments.

Marilyn told us in a group session that she was very excited to have met a man on Match.com. "He owns his own company, is quite wealthy, has been divorced for ten years and owns a home on the water in Martha's Vineyard." She went on to say he was 63 years old and he looked older than his age but "so what, I think I really like him."

The "so what" was not very convincing; Marilyn is not overly materialistic although appearance means a great deal to her. As you read about her story, you can understand her longing and her dilemma. She longs for someone who can give her financial security for the first time in her adult life. Roger has this capacity, but the problem is that her PA is about appearance. She describes her ex as a Tom Selleck look-alike. You see the problem!

Marilyn is going to realize sooner rather than later, particularly because she attends group sessions, that this relationship is based on a longing that Roger cannot satisfy. She thinks she needs financial security and a handsome man, when what she really needs is to change her belief system about her own aging appearance and go back to the story that says she needs to be taken care of by a man.

Despite years of supporting herself and her family, she still talks as if she can't make her way in the world. After years of believing her looks are the main attraction to a man, she is aging and increasingly feeling less worthy. She remains quite attractive, but her story has yet to be unraveled so she can see herself clearly and ultimately make a choice in a man with open eyes. Marilyn remains confused about the value of appearance and she is in doubt as to how to find security and true love in the same man.

Real Love with a Real Person

Nick, a real estate agent and ten years younger than Marilyn, exhibits a different kind of longing—a healthy longing based on two years of therapy and an intense involvement in AA. Nick is a recovering alcoholic who is in the process of being divorced from his wife of the same age (45.)

When I met him, he was newly sober, his business was hurting and his wife, "a beautiful owner of a wellness center and a fitness fanatic," was asking for a divorce as she was involved with a body builder who worked out at her gym. Nick discovered the affair shortly before he started seeing me and was devastated.

He told me several times during our first meeting about his wife's beauty and how successful she has been in her business. He clearly felt guilty for not being as productive and knew his alcoholism during their marriage had seriously compromised his ability to perform. He brought her to the subsequent meeting and yes, she was quite attractive, articulate, but also quite narcissistic and self-promoting.

He begged her to not leave him, to give up the affair with the 27-year-old, but she refused. He ran out of my office, slamming the door and threatened suicide.

We met the following week and I told him I could see how very devastated he was and I also saw how he viewed Regina as his judge and jury. I mentioned that it was dangerous to turn over one's sense of self exclusively to any one person, no matter who they are.

After expressing these thoughts, I told him I wanted to help him, but I could not tolerate the outburst of last week. He agreed and from that time on, he has been remarkably committed to healing. For months he came to weekly sessions religiously, got an AA sponsor, attended five meeting per week and today, on the verge of finalizing the end of his marriage, he is a much more resilient person.

Nick's problem stems from his first few years of life. Hi mother died when he was six. He was then raised by his maternal aunt and uncle, seldom seeing his father, who remarried when he was nine and had two additional children by his second wife. His father moved to a town one and a half hours away and steadily lost interest in keeping in touch with Nick during this critical time in his life.

Nick began drinking at age fourteen and hung out with "older guys in the neighborhood who treated me like their little brother." He got into cocaine, pain killers and weed in his senior year in high school and, despite being accepted to college, his alcohol and drug use led to him dropping out after his freshman year.

He met Regina at a club in Manhattan. She was a "preppy who liked a good time but kind of took me under her wing and taught me how to behave in social situations." They lived together while she finished her business degree at NYU and married thereafter. Regina served as the mother substitute since Nick's longing was for a woman to take care of him, nurture him and give him self-esteem. He is a small man of slight build and always considered himself that "guy who couldn't get the pretty girl." So being able to date and marry Regina was a wish-come-true for him.

Regina admitted to me that she gets into trouble with people all the time by becoming overly-involved. "I know I mother people. I don't set limits and then I resent being used. Nick has been leaching off me all our married life. We have two daughters and Nick is the third baby in the family."

I only met with Regina and Nick on three occasions. She quit thereafter, saying it was useless. Regina refused to address the affair, saying it was none of his business and that she finally was having some fun in her life.

Nick has always had a rather idealistic view of women, thinking that if he could be with a "beauty," he would compensate for his view of himself as less than handsome. As we worked together, he increasingly impressed me with an emerging view of women that seemed deeper as he began to think more of himself.

As he began to manage his life less impulsively, and handled conflict more directly and assertively (without drugs or any acting out behavior,) his sense of self became increasingly stable. He gradually became less doubtful, his business picked up and only months ago he met an old high school friend returning from the West coast where she had lived for several years.

Maria is also divorced and the mother of twin, nine-year-old daughters. She is not the typical kind of woman with whom Nick would become enamored. She is attractive, but not an eye opener. She is a bit overweight, but most importantly, when Nick re-engaged with her, she told him she was suffering from a rare form of cancer than has been fatal in most cases.

Surprising her medical team, after eight months of treatment, she is tolerating chemo and radiation and her tumors are shrinking. More surprising is that Nick has fallen in love with her and has told her that he will be with her "every step of the way." He has changed from a man focused on the superficial aspects of a person to compensate for his low self-esteem—into to a man longing for a sound, committed relationship based on truly knowing the object of his love.

This transition is the beginning of a deeper path to intimacy rather than the unsatisfying longing for an image that provides immediate relief and ultimate dissatisfaction.

Nick is feeling so much better about himself. He has entered a relationship on a much more mature level than ever before. He is able to be with a woman whose life is at risk, who is not perfect looking, but who is a person of quality and character that Nick has come to value immensely. He has moved from image love to real love.

Is Your Story Creating Longings in You?

You have seen how each of my clients, at different ages, has been ruled by particular longings. As you have learned in these examples, you don't have to feel helpless to alter your deepest desires. When you are open to looking at the origins of your novel and changing the story you created through genuine relationship with others, you have the power to set yourself free.

Questions to Journal:

- Whether you are married, single, or divorced, are you aware of what your relationship longings are at this moment?

- Do you realize what is missing in your relationships? Do you use this awareness as a cue to work on the missing ingredient before expecting someone else to satisfy the need?

- Can you tell the difference between a healthy and unhealthy longing?

- Have you identified the typical love drives you have that are mostly an attempt to remedy your ill feeling toward yourself, rather than being driven toward healthy connections with other people? What are they?

- Do you think you know how to move beyond the surface with someone to whom you're attracted? If not, what interferes?

- Do you think you can maintain meaningful intimacy over time?

- If not, what are the reasons that stop you from having long-term love of a high quality?

- What, to you, are the key ingredients in a meaningful love relationship? Have you had the experience of in-depth love, really knowing the other's character and loving him/her for his/her constitution?

- If not, what do you think prevents you from having this experience?

- What are the images that most influence you initially in a potential love relationship?

- What do those perceptions tell you about yourself?

Get Grounded in Experience

1. If constant chatter is keeping intimacy at bay, or if you are using any other method to keep people in your life at arm's length, then at some point during the process of reading this book, with a spouse, friend or family member, share an intimate moment by disclosing an aspect of your journal that is particularly revealing and related to your difficulties with closeness.

2. Record in your journal the particular emotional trials that most interfere with your ability to maintain intimacy. Make a commitment to revisit those trials until you feel free of their negative impact.

Chapter 12:
Winning the Balancing Act—
Exceptional Mediocrity

Are you trying to be exceptional, but forgetting what it means to be extra ordinary? The space between the words "extra" and "ordinary" is not a grammatical error. When you are truly extra ordinary, you are naturally exceptional, but when you try to be exceptional, overlooking what is ordinary and bypassing the common needs we all have, you become anything but exceptional.

Trying to be exceptional at the cost of overlooking everyday fundamentals, attentive interactions with those around you and other acts of living successfully and joyfully, is a sure sign of the deeper issues you've learned about in earlier chapters.

Remember, performance addiction cloaked as the need to achieve incessantly is one of the biggest cover-ups of our time. It's reinforced by our culture because of its economic benefits and the rewards attached, but by no means are you exceptional when you don't have a strong basis in the core tenets of successful living. This is a common plight in the life of anyone suffering from *the curse*, particularly those who are highly PA.

An Easy Distortion in Thinking

Distortions in thinking are accompanied by misperceptions. Not understanding the distinction between exceptional and extraordinary can cause a myriad of problems. I am, of course, not saying that having exceptional skills or abilities is going to automatically cause undue pressure that will lead to dysfunction.

Michael Phelps is one of the greatest Olympians of all time. He has an exceptional ability to swim like a swordfish, yet he is also extra ordinary at the same time. If he tried to be the best at everything, he would be plagued with problems.

Life becomes problematic when we attempt to be exceptional in all areas. Consequently, we end up not appreciating the ordinary pleasures that don't require so much work—that don't require "achievement." It is often very difficult for achievers or those obsessed with achievement, to allow themselves joy, if they have not worked for it. If it just happens, it doesn't feel quite right!

I Don't Want to be Mediocre

This chapter was written because I noticed repeatedly in group coaching sessions that achievers often mention their distaste for the word *mediocre*. These are people who have an inordinate fear of being "average" in their performance or appearance. They want to excel. They don't want to be an "average Joe" as one of my clients frequently indicates.

I also noticed in these meetings that people preoccupied with achievement seem to minimize the daily things we need to do to maintain balance, health and well-being. They see acts and behaviors that don't attract much attention as the aspects of life that are not noteworthy.

I often ask my clients who they know who maintains balance in the five essential areas of self care: **sleep, nutrition, exercise, meaningful work and relationships**. As you might expect, people seldom mention more than one person and most people say they don't know anyone with balance in each of these areas.

I created the term *exceptional mediocrity* to accent the rare achiever who actually succeeds in all five areas on most days. *Mediocre* is not a favorable term in the minds of most people because it means being ordinary, yet in the absurdity of our quest to be exceptional, we don't get the benefit of our common needs being fulfilled.

In today's cultural climate, it is truly amazing when an individual can manage to attend to these five dynamics with consistency. Achievers and people with PA in particular, don't tend to value success in these seemingly low-level abilities. (They usually accent the work category as the area of most relevance and of highest value.)

After all, who cares if you eat nutritionally or exercised today as long as you're putting numbers on the board? Who cares if you left your home with a sweet feeling between you and your spouse on the way to the airport as long as you get the contract signed on the West Coast?

The answer is not many. Few hard-driving people will express concern for others in any of these self-care areas because taking care of oneself or others is seen as a less important, secondary agenda. Many people won't admit they actually feel this way, but ask their significant others and they will tell you behavior speaks for itself.

UN-exceptional

I have a client who is an avid cyclist, completed a 146-mile ride just a few weekends ago and is doing the Pan Mass Challenge again this year. She is a buyer for a major clothing line, travels weekly and recently returned from a ten day trip to China. She is divorced and has two adult children—one is a school teacher and another is a sophomore in college. For the past eight years, she has been in a relationship with a man. She is quite attractive and has an aerobic capacity that is rare for a woman of age 46.

Emily called me a year ago from Europe. She was reading *Performance Addiction* on her flight (at the suggestion of a friend,) and was particularly affected by a chapter titled "Exceptional Mediocrity."

Emily is an unusual individual in many ways. For instance, she is not a college graduate, yet she has risen up the corporate ladder over the years. All the people she oversees have business degrees and have gone through a rigorous training program for two years before actually beginning field work.

She is a dedicated mother and, by all accounts, her son and daughter are exceptional people. Her employer thinks very highly of her and additionally expects her to often work late, travel frequently and be extremely committed to the business. She doesn't have friends, is isolated socially and her only involvement outside of work is with the man she sees weekly when she is home. She exercises rigorously on weekends, but her workouts are often canceled during the week due to travel and working until late in the evening.

Unlike most people, she loves to exercise but can't seem to establish a regular schedule with all the other demands on her time. So what's so bad about this picture? As you will see, Emily's exceptional way of life is devoid of extraordinary. She's not experiencing the benefits of getting her true needs met, including that of having enough time to simply rejuvenate.

Rushing to her Demise

I wish I could just show you a video of Emily hurrying into group one week. Her entrance is generally the same. She is late, stuck in traffic at Logan airport, the plane was not on time or her boss kept her late wanting to know what happened on her last business trip. She looks harried, depleted and overwhelmed.

She tries to hold it together in our sessions, making jokes and trying to make it seem like her lifestyle works. It doesn't. In the midst of her traveling and working late, she cycles long distances on the weekend, then gets up at 4:30 a.m. Monday morning to make an early flight and so goes her life. She is quite intelligent and can't understand why, at the end of every week, she is so rundown.

The man she lives with is friendly, somewhat self-centered, has his own problems with PA and works most weekends in his real estate business. He doesn't understand why Emily can't manage the travel like "everyone else in the business."

Emily knows he believes she could manage her time better and she knows he believes she should be grateful to be making so much money and to be so highly regarded. "After all," as he says, "in this economy there are few people in your position, especially without a business degree. "Where are you going to go at age 46 and make the same money?" Stanley is sharing his view of success with Emily.

He came to a session with her recently and gave her his very best advice. "Look, you can't give up. You can't complain about the hours worked, or the travel. You're making money. You're at the top of your company. What else do you want? You're a success and everybody we know envies you. You just have to set more limits with people and you'll start to feel better."

I asked Stanley to tell me exactly how Emily could "set limits and feel better." The discussion then became vague and illogical. I think this happened because he can't understand a way of life that seems like the life of a "loser" to him. If you're making money and are well-regarded in the corporate world, you're a winner. Anything else pales in comparison. Perhaps her schedule and earnings works for him, but not for her!

Consumed by Her Story

Emily's ex-husband had two affairs before she asked for a divorce. He lives on the West Coast and sees his children, on average, once a year. She doesn't see herself as being able to attract men and feels humiliated by what happened in her marriage. She would be incredibly frightened to be in the world without Stanley. After all, his *pathological certainty* counters her self-doubt and at times she feels comforted by the fact that Stanley always seems to have the answers.

Can you imagine what her internal story is, the one she tells herself each day? The war stories and success stories she shares with others cover up what's really going on for her.

You may be thinking: this is a woman who travels to China to scout new factories, buys for a major player in the clothing business and she's afraid to be without Stanley? Remember that success in the business world is seldom correlated to the world of love and romance.

Emily is also frustrated by her inability to lose weight despite her avid cycling on weekends. She often eats poorly on the road or when she is stressed at home, which is most of the time. She is very sensitive about aging and is afraid she is losing more of her appeal. She is worried about all the young kids coming into the business who have more energy and better training, at least according to Emily.

Most importantly, Emily has never seen the self-care aspects of life as crucial to her existence. She can always eat better tomorrow and make up for not exercising during the week on the weekend. She can catch up on her sleep on the plane and can make up for forgetting her mother's birthday by getting her a great gift from India on her next trip.

She misses her niece's and nephew's birthday parties, has lost touch with old friends and yet complains that her social network is very shallow. Her only friends are work connections that are not based on genuine caring.

There is no secret why Emily is overweight—it's her lifestyle, how she is thinking (the story she is telling herself; the real one she is not sharing with others,) and how she is living. And until she changes her view of herself and ultimately her lifestyle, it will mean more of the same.

Praying for a Way Out!

Many of the important aspects of Emily's life have been shoved into the background. Yet when she gets a call from her mother and hears the disappointment in her voice, she feels guilty.

Emily lives with a great deal of guilt and, as she often says, "I can't pull it all off—work, home, family, exercise, eating. It's just too much. Sometimes I honestly fantasize about the plane crashing, just as a way out. I know it sounds crazy, but I can't figure out how to save my life, how to meet everyone's needs and how to be happy. I haven't felt happy in years."

Emily is just beginning to realize the value of the aspects of a life she and Stanley consider mediocre, thus the paradox of exceptional mediocrity. It is truly exceptional to be able to consistently eat a nutritionally sound diet, exercise regularly, foster your relationships, do meaningful work effectively and sleep enough hours. But each of the five areas makes the other possible. They are interrelated and self-care is the foundation for a healthy lifestyle. For some people, however, the regular attention to these foundations of life seems far too regular.

The Same Old Story

Emily has longed to be loved for so long that she has been trying to be everything for everybody. These pressures have made life a burden of monumental proportions. She keeps relying on the same old theory with the same negative results.

Of course, every now and then she pulls it all off, she is applauded and she finally feels good for a short time. But she wakes up the next morning knowing she has to do it all over again and she immediately feels overwhelmed.

Not knowing any other way, she tries harder and harder to reach a level of accomplishment that will finally quiet the negative voice in her head. She is using the only tools she has, but she has the wrong map with no other directional assistance.

Peel the layers back and it's the same old story that developed early in her life. This led to performance addiction and her drive to prove herself worthy. All the emotional trials came as a result of a lack of balance and well-being, underpinned by the downward trend of being overwhelmed, exhausted and fatigued. You can see why Emily suffers from this distortion in thinking. Emily is living like so many accomplished people in our society; with great stress and a limited awareness of what prevents her from living a healthy lifestyle.

To date she's never had a forum to gain the understanding necessary to resolve her pronounced PA and to gain freedom from the persistent, unrelenting perfectionism she has believed would bring her satisfaction and peace of mind. She has unknowingly devalued self-care and does not understand how critical the extraordinary aspects of a healthy lifestyle are for exceptional achievement.

The fundamentals of self-care are the core of successful living and the fuel for sustainable personal and professional success. Our society devalues behavior that is considered to be ordinary and overvalues behavior that is media-worthy, yet superficial in nature. But neither Emily, nor you, needs to buy into the hardwiring of the past any longer.

Your Personal Foundation

Although Emily is a new member of the group process, she is gaining insights every week. Regardless of the fact that she has felt hurt by the feedback she has received, she is building her personal foundation. She comes back week after week, trying to understand what she has to learn and what she needs to unlearn to begin living with more joy and balance.

She is coachable and, because of her desire to get free, she will eventually clear the road to internal calm, while at the same time developing the resilient sense of self that she really needs. The path must include acceptance of the ordinary as neither a reflection of her being "less than" or "more than."

You must develop emotional, psychological and physical stability and strength the same way all other healthy human beings do, with the humble acceptance that we human beings need to establish self-care as the foundation of our lives. Sustaining our capabilities depends on this basic truth.

Questions to Journal:

- Do you value the aspects of self-care that are not necessarily noticeable to the social world? For instance, no one will know if you exercised today or if you ate in a healthy manner. If these behaviors do not get you applause in the world, do you devalue their importance?

- Do you recognize when you are tired, need rest and should go to sleep? Do you push ahead, cleaning the house, answering emails, etc. until exhaustion makes you stop? Why?

- Do you recognize when you're hungry? Do you have regular times when you eat?

- Do you go past a normal period of eating and even take pride in letting your coworkers know you were so busy you didn't have time to eat? What purpose does this serve?

- Do you secretly tally how many hours you work and derive pleasure from letting people know how very busy you have been?

- Do you credit how hard you work as a prideful experience that gives you an edge over others?

- Do you consider coworkers who take time off to go to a movie with one of their children to be a slacker?

- Do you think of the words *mediocre* and *average* as descriptions that would be extremely distasteful to you?

- Do you believe your conditioning makes it mandatory that you excel beyond others in certain categories or you will feel deflated?

- Can you explain why you answered yes to any of the preceding questions?

- How many people do you know who maintain balance in the five areas of self-care? Which areas to do you value most? Which do you value the least?

Get Grounded in Experience

1. Just be unexceptional for a day. Make no new commitments. Allow others to take on responsibilities you would naturally assume and experience how living in balance can be relaxing and fun!

2. Notice how it feels to have a conversation without attempting to establish your merit or trying to impress. Confront your fear of being ordinary in the presence of another.

3. Let those close to you in on your fear of not being good enough. Realize this behavior is extra ordinary!

Chapter 13:
It's Not All About You –
The Barriers to Empathy

Thinking *it's all about you* is a distortion in thinking. Empathy is the core skill to overcoming just about every aspect of *the curse*. Having genuine relationships with others is the path to developing a new story for personal freedom.

If you are not in an intimate relationship centered on empathy with others, what's left but to be self-absorbed? When you are self-absorbed, chronically caught up in your achievements, engaging in small talk, deflective and constantly giving advice, you are not truly relating.

The Key to Intimacy and Trust

If you are going to be successful in life, personally and professionally, it is absolutely essential that you develop the capacity for empathy to its full extent. Empathy, the capacity to understand and respond to the unique experiences of another, is the key to managing the mine field of the interpersonal world.

Empathy is also a great aid in assessing diverse situations. It is our guide to reading and relating to other people of all persuasions in life. Understanding the value of empathy in your life is the first step in being able to use this capacity to attain a higher level of well-being. It is also the place where a supportive story is developed—where you get involved in the lives of others and inspire others to get involved in yours.

Empathy guides us in determining who to trust and who to remain distant from. It allows us to read beyond the surface and determine the truth in any situation or with any person. Unlike sympathy and compassion, it is objective, present-oriented and always focused on the unique rather than the general.

When empathy is not present, it is harder to trust, for the fear of judgment looms large. Hence, it is critical to our health. It reduces tension, builds confidence and lessens the release of stress hormones. In due course, it reinforces the ability to develop deep relationships.

The Key to High Achievement

Empathy, which widens the lens with which we see the world and allows us to expand our connections beyond what is familiar to us, is all about relating and relating accurately. Once you realize that, without a diligent effort to improve your empathic potential you will be leading a limited life. Most people begin the process of wanting to know what expands a person's empathic range. It is essential for high achievement and a corresponding feeling of success.

It is not enough to know what enhances empathy. It is equally and possibly more important to know what inhibits its development. Knowing what does not work usually translates to what does, or at least points us in a different direction.

Since I wrote *The Power of Empathy* in 2000, there have been several research studies and texts explaining its value and how to hone in on improving this skill. We now know this ability can be taught.

I have personally witnessed this progression many times over the years in my group programs. I have seen individuals who have been self-absorbed and labeled as having "little empathy," emerge over time with an advanced ability to understand and respond to complex experiences that demand advanced interpersonal skill.

There has not been much attention given to the barriers to empathy and how to remove them. Much of what has been written recently focuses on the discovery of where empathy and compassion are located in the brain and how we may possess empathy neurons, but little attention has been paid to what actually diminishes empathy—thus the focus of this chapter.

The Balance of Listening

One of the most profound hindrances to the development of empathy is poor listening skills. It is crucial to be aware of your style of talking and interacting. I have seen hundreds of professional people enter group therapy and not realize how bored others are as they are go on in dramatic fashion about themselves, their expertise and their achievements. Some don't even read the cues of the disenchanted faces right in front of them.

When you're speaking, look at the person you're addressing. If you want to know if what you're saying is interesting or not, all the feedback you need is before you. When you are talking on the phone, check in with the listener to see how they perceive you.

Ask questions like, "Do you want me to go on? What are you thinking about what I just said?" Also, when you call someone, ask them if they can talk, or if it's a good time to converse. Don't assume because you're calling, they're waiting to hear from you.

People with narcissistic tendencies seldom realize they could say what they mean with far fewer words. Their need to be at the center of a conversation tends to make them long-winded. Remember that, whether you're writing or speaking, fewer words with succinct meaning are far more appealing. If you traditionally talk more than you listen, you are cutting off the potential for an empathic interchange.

And remember, it's not empathic to just listen to someone go on and on while you're saying to yourself, "Does she have any idea she told me this all before?" It is empathic to interrupt if the person characteristically does not come up for air and say, "I really don't like interrupting but, before you continue, I wanted you to know you already told me this story." You're giving the person truthful feedback in a tactful way. That is empathy.

Being passive with someone who is narcissistic is not empathic. They need feedback and most often they probably don't receive it, since narcissistic people tend to be fragile and defensive. As a result, people tread lightly with them, depriving both parties of potential growth.

You will be surprised that if you're tactful and your intention is not to be hurtful, you may be received with gratefulness (since few people dare to give a narcissistic person honest feedback.) It will develop your emotional fitness to provide feedback rathcr than to come to conclusions about a person and cut off the potential for a relationship of substance.

Empathic conversations have to be give-and-take. Ask yourself if your interactions seem to be equal or if one party dominates most often. Ask yourself if you are truly interested in the person you're talking to, or just looking to attain something for yourself.

If you know how to listen and give of yourself, you will always attract people. It never fails. In conversations, remember to consider the flow between you and the other. Do you use ten sentences to your companion's three? Is it the other way around? Where is the equality of interchange? Start to keep track and see what your style reveals about you and your needs.

The Power of Group Feedback

In a session the other day, a member who is fairly new to the group process was telling us about himself, his driven nature and his anxiety. He was describing his work environment, his family of origin, his marriage and, as he talked, people were asking questions.

I could see that he felt satisfied with their ongoing interest. I asked at one point how it was that no one has mentioned to Robert that he was repeating the same information he had given us the past four weeks.

A silence ensued. Robert then said, "I was trying to learn more about my anxiety, why I feel uncomfortable with people and why I often feel like I don't measure up."

I said that I believed that was his intent, but I noticed that in four weeks, he had repeated basically the same information. But when others talked, he seemed far less interested and hadn't asked questions or re-acted much to what they had said.

It is difficult for Robert. He is truly unhappy, but his way of engaging is to mostly talk about himself. He is in his own head too often and for too long. He can't help but be preoccupied because he is troubled. This is quite understandable.

However, he is going to learn more about himself by entering into relationships with other people rather than intellectualizing about his life in our presence. Now, for people accustomed to this approach, they find it difficult to understand, at least initially, that this manner of interact-ing greatly limits empathic interchange. He longs for understanding, but guess what? He doesn't usually get what he's after. *If you don't give it, you're not likely to receive it for very long.*

Self-absorption is a natural tendency when we are troubled, but it is also a relational style for many people. It is especially so for people ob-sessed with their own image. They tend to forget or overlook the person on the other side of the table.

It is understandable to be self-focused on specific, unique occasions. If you were laid off yesterday, just found out your husband is having an affair with the next-door neighbor or are excited about an achievement, I would expect you to be very preoccupied. This is a chance for someone else to be empathic with you. But when it is a standard way of communi-cating, it is an empathy killer.

Hiding Behind Your Story

In the case of Robert, he learns much less by going over and over his history than by participating in an interaction. As you know from our earlier accent on the novel, it is necessary to understand our history in order to understand ourselves completely. However, when our history becomes an exclusive way of understanding oneself, it can be a perva-sive defense. In other words it is a means of telling people about your-self rather than being in actual interactions where people can decide for themselves who you are by how you act, respond and relate in real time.

The telling, about yourself to excess is a control issue and one that seems protective in nature, but ultimately prevents personal growth. We learn much more by giving and receiving feedback in conversations with others.

It is like the person who recently told us upon joining group that he is very giving, but after six months of sessions, fails to demonstrate any substantial caring for others. In his own mind, he believes he is giving (a subjective conclusion.) In reality, the objective facts do not agree with the view he had internally. This is a common occurrence.

The Safety of Giving a Monologue

I have met with Robert for several months in individual sessions and have found he can easily talk about himself, with little reaction from me, for fifty minutes. He actually seems like he is entertained by his own thought pattern, often laughing when he believes he has made a noteworthy discovery regarding his behavior.

Once I intervene, however, I can see how easily he becomes anxious. Suddenly, he does not know where the conversation is going and will try to return to the monologue where he feels safe and in control. He is not intending to be non-reciprocal, but it is the only way he knows to try to help himself.

Robert was referred to me by his Human Resources department at work because he has trouble understanding and reacting to the concerns of those in his department. He is a manager without the interpersonal skills to make others feel heard and, as a result, his relationships with his colleagues suffer. His wife and children also complain. His adolescent son told him that a conversation with him is like watching Jay Leno do a monologue.

So, in essence, it doesn't help Robert and he cannot improve in understanding others if we let him simply live in his head in our presence. He wants to learn and, with gentle guidance, I believe he will begin relating, become more in tune with the conversation and experience more pleasure (as we all do when we are empathically connected.) In the short time Robert has been in group his interpersonal style has changed from being self preoccupied to being empathically connected to other members. The resultant change in his spirit and energy level is quite apparent.

The Everyday Barriers

One's inability to be intimate is not always the result of early develop-ment, addictions or emotional trials. There are practical matters in the present that can block this way of being and relating.

We live in busy times and there is a lot going on, usually related to accomplishing tasks and achievement. Too many tasks without enough support are an empathy-killer.

Are you caught up with work yet unable to relate with others? Is your constant busyness standing in the way of genuine relating?

Balanced, healthy achievement in life naturally requires genuine relationships with others. Rest, recovery, relaxation and spiritual rejuve-nation come from a different mode of exchange.

Be careful about buying into the mode of the times. Highly capable people can easily default to time management. Energy management strategies can cut off the very juice of life—relating with others. In the process, they reinforce the very pattern they want to eliminate. As with any area of taking care of yourself, it has to happen in the process of achievement, not simply after the fact. Remember it isn't always about you. You can take care of you by getting involved with others.

Work It Out

Empathy is like a muscle; if you don't use your inherent capacity to understand others and the situation around you accurately, it diminishes. It can be enhanced through practice or it will wither through an over-preoccupation with yourself and your needs. Even though you may have a need to be absorbed in the moment, a great exercise is to immerse yourself in the experience of another or the awareness of what's going on around you.

First of all, it will almost seem like a break from the story playing in your head—the one you have been telling yourself for some time, perhaps years. It will also be an exercise in flexibility, to be able to shift the mode you are in and change gears.

Remember there is a major distinction between *empathic* listening and *sympathetic* listening. Empathy is an innate capacity that motivates us to acts of compassion and altruism. Sympathy is an emotion, the passive experience of sharing another person's fear, grief, sorrow, etc. Empathy is focused on the unique experiences of another, while sympathy is focused on the general and non-specific, and thus is not tailor-made to the individual.

Sympathy and compassion are usually immediate reactions attempting to console, while empathy goes beyond "I feel for you" to "I understand you." Sympathetic listening assumes, through immediate identification, that we know what another is experiencing. Empathy, on the other hand, makes no such assumption.

In essence, empathic listening is more objective, never assuming, "I know exactly how you feel," and always taking the position of going deeper in an attempt to understand the heart and soul of another.

If you can learn to listen from this perspective, you have eliminated the greatest possibilities of creating empathy barriers. The empathic muscle takes time and patience to develop. Empathic fitness is no less challenging than physical fitness.

Time to Change

Thinking it's all about you is a distortion in thinking. You now know its origin. Yet because you may have suffered from this distortion for some time, it may have become solidified in your personality. It has become an ingrained pattern.

Like any other distortion, this way of being will take time to change. Don't be discouraged if you revert back to sympathetic listening. Just consciously decide to understand someone before claiming to know how he or she feels.

As you exercise this muscle daily, you will see it becoming more natural for you to be thinking empathetically.

Questions to Journal:

- How would you classify your relational style? Are you a listener or a talker? Explain.

- Do you slant the scale on one side or the other, or do you adapt your style to the situation at hand?

- Are you impatient when you meet with a friend or colleague when you realize he or she expects to converse reciprocally and you cannot dominate the conversation with your own needs? How come?

- Do you tend to listen more than you speak? If so, are you in this mode for positive reasons or is it a way of hiding behind being in the caretaker role?

- Do you understand the difference between empathy and sympathy? Explain.

- Do you experience empathy when listening but have trouble knowing how to put your experience into words?

- Do you understand the role of empathy in real love vs. image love? Explain.

- Do you understand the role of empathy in your sexual life?

- What comes to mind when you think of immersing yourself in an empathic interchange with someone close to you?

- Do you believe that you have developed a high capacity for empathy? Explain. If not, describe what has interfered.

- Do you find it difficult to experience empathy for those unlike yourself? How come?

- Do you experience empathy for people suffering in other countries or do you confine your expression of empathy to those you know directly?

- Do you have empathy for those who hurt you in the past? What can't you understand about their actions?

- Could you have empathy for those people who seem to be without mercy for others, such as terrorists, or is this question stretching your empathic range too far?

Get Grounded in Experience

1. At your earliest opportunity, engage in what's usually a difficult conversation with another person with the express intention of trying to understand their unique experience. Try to not defend your usual story or way of being. Just listen, ask questions and relate. Make sure you're focused on understanding rather than problem solving!

2. Listen empathically and reduce the time you spend rehearsing your response. Notice what comes up for you when you're not preoccupied with trying to make your point.

Chapter 14:
How to Be What the Situation Calls for— The Dimmer Switch

In the previous chapter, we addressed the inability to use empathy to understand others and accurately access situations. The barriers to empathy are costly and don't enable you to know how or when to turn the emotional and intellectual dial up or down. You remain stuck in one gear and, as a result, you remain at a significant disadvantage on many fronts in life.

From inability to manage your personal energy to interpersonal interactions, learning how to turn down the dial to fit the situation is a dilemma many achievers encounter. Learning when to turn your emotional dial up or down can dramatically help you improve your ability to relate to others.

Turn Down the Dial

Most driven achievers don't have an internal mechanism that allows them to control their intensity to decide when it does not fit the situation they are currently encountering. They live with a certain amount of tension, whether they are in a tense situation or not. They are so often worried about performance that they can't, or don't know how, to control their emotions. They have no dimmer switch.

Have you ever gone to dinner at a friend's house, eaten in her dining room where she had no dimmer switch on the chandelier? It makes the whole night a bit uncomfortable and you end up wishing there was a softer light in the room.

Who needs this much light especially as the sun sets and the people at the table are trying to relax? This is how individuals without a dimmer switch feel internally most of the time. The lights don't dim and, even in their sleep, they wake up and turn on immediately.

In fact, many people without a dimmer switch do not sleep soundly; once they wake up, they can't go back to sleep because they are already back in the saddle, worrying about what they have to do tomorrow.

Why is this so? Unresolved issues and unmet needs lead to less internal calm. Once again, if unresolved emotional issues accumulate, self-preservation kicks in and emotions must be covered up or at least quelled in order to perform. For many, the mechanism to cope creates incessant intensity that comes with the endless pace of accomplishment and achievement.

The Type-A Personality

We have all heard of the Type-A personality. Type-A "Achiever" personalities purportedly struggle with balance and well-being because of the intensity with which they live every day.

This 60-year-old research has been widely popularized and also widely criticized for its scientific shortcomings. The Type-A and Type-B personality theory is a theory that describes a pattern of behaviors that were once considered to be a risk factor for coronary heart disease.

Type-A individuals can be described as having strong achievement-orientation, being impatient, excessively time-conscious, insecure about their status and highly competitive. They are, at times hostile, aggressive and incapable of relaxation. They also develop certain physical characteristics that result from the excessive stress of so-called Type-A behavior over a period of years.

Physical Symptoms:

- Facial Tension (Tight Lips, Clenched Jaw, etc.)

- Tongue Clicking or Teeth Grinding

- Dark Circles under Eyes

- Facial Sweating (On Forehead or Upper Lip)

They are often high-achieving workaholics who multi-task, drive themselves with deadlines and are unhappy about the smallest of delays. Because of these characteristics, Type A individuals are often described as "stress junkies."

Type-B individuals, in contrast, are described as patient, relaxed and easy-going. There is also a **Type-AB** mixed profile for people who cannot be clearly categorized.

In his 1996 book, *Type A Behavior: Its Diagnosis and Treatment*, Meyer Friedman suggests that Type A behavior is expressed in three major symptoms. One of these symptoms is believed to be covert and therefore less observable, whereas the other two are more overt.

Behavioral Symptoms of Type-A Behavior

1. An intrinsic insecurity or feeling of inadequacy, insufficient level of self-esteem or poor self image, which is considered to be the root cause of the syndrome. This is believed to be hidden and out of view (*the curse.*)

2. Constant time pressure and edginess, which causes irritation and desperation.

3. "Free floating" hostility, which can be triggered by even minor incidents.

Defined by Your Story

The symptoms above do not indicate that there are underlying issues that are driving your behavior. Type-A behavior is the end result of deeper, unresolved issues. It is your story that is reinforcing this type of lifestyle. The label describes symptoms that lead to personality classification without a comprehensive understanding of the individual and the causes of his or her driven nature.

In the beginning of this book, I noted that high achievers are such forward-moving people that they often are excellent at covering up their past. Their ambition outpaces their ability to take care of themselves. This is essentially what's been taking place in their life for a long time and it can manifest as Type-A behavior.

In the midst of anticipating an exciting future (when you are likely to continue to attain positive outcomes,) the ability to take care of yourself is obviously much easier to manage. Just look at athletes, for example. In a healthy mindset, they have the ability to turn up or turn down the intensity on call for optimal performance.

But watch what happens when the fear of negative consequences comes into play. They will often over train and overcompensate the same way everyday achievers will overwork. Since people will do more to avoid negative consequences of the past, it's easier to see why they will drive themselves incessantly toward the future.

We explain our behavior in life by the stories we create. If you say you are a Type-A personality, your lifestyle and behavior will likely follow. It sounds like *a curse* to label yourself as such, because many Type-A people are overwhelmed, exhausted, fatigued, overweight and suffering from the health complications that are the byproducts of driven behavior.

Labels are Generalities

Interestingly, in recent years, researchers have postulated several types of personalities that reportedly contribute to certain diseases.

The perfectionist personality has been linked to rheumatoid arthritis; the compliant personality to migraines and stomach disorders; the anxious personality to alcohol abuse, etc. In psychiatrist David Servan-Schrieber's wonderful book, *Anti-Cancer*, he cites the work of various psychologists and psychiatrists who have conducted research confirming the Type-C (cancer) personality.

Servan-Schrieber, a cancer survivor himself, highlights the cancer personality as a person who did not feel welcome in childhood, seldom shows anger and is frequently described as a "saint" by others, while tending to over-invest in a single aspect of his/her life. These individuals are labeled as personalities prone to cancer proliferation.

Research studies that label personalities in such general ways can be helpful and also hurtful. We certainly don't want someone recently diagnosed with cancer to feel guilty when they may have done nothing to cause the disease to flourish.

On the other hand, these research studies offer clues to what we may need to do to change and maintain our health. Dr. Servan-Schrieber's book, for instance, is an excellent nutritional resource for cancer prevention and overall health.

Over the years, I have paid very close attention to people who achieve on very high levels, are exceptional in their professions and are well-respected; yet lead balanced, healthy lives with high levels of intimacy. They are essentially extra ordinary, as we have detailed in the previous chapter. One study stands out in my mind in this regard as it made such a huge impression on me several years ago.

Dr. Kenneth Pelletier, a Stanford medical school psychologist specializing in disease prevention, conducted a five year study of fifty-three prominent individuals who excelled in their careers. They were regarded as prominent in their professional lives. The group consisted of corporate presidents, a Nobel Prize laureate in physics, composers, editors, US senators, actors and actresses and Hollywood producers.

All these individuals, twenty-one women and thirty-two men, could be easily viewed as Type-A personalities from afar. My interest was piqued, however, by the fact that each individual in "The Sound Mind-Sound Body" study met the required criterion of being regarded as extremely successful in business or his/her chosen profession. They adhered to personal health practices and were all motivated by a strong sense of purpose or higher spiritual values.

Dr. Pelletier was inspired by the groundbreaking work of noted American psychologist Abraham Maslow, who he cited as wanting to study "the extraordinary to understand the ordinary" in self-actualized people. Dr. Pelletier thus chose to study individuals who retain balance and yet are high achievers. Valuing the ordinary aspects of life establishes the foundation for solid, self-resiliency and outstanding achievement.

Pelletier and Maslow were both interested in studying these exceptional achievers who, in many ways, were quite ordinary. They had the same struggles as the average person and, in many cases, they had suffered great disappointment and tragedy. Many had suffered childhood trauma and, of note, they all had been greatly influenced by their fathers in their development, each citing a need to meet the demands of their strong fathers.

Another key ingredient in the lives of these high achievers was spending time overcoming past hurts. This allowed them to live in balance. They rewrote their story with an objective pen and continued to live life without resentment from the past. They all moved beyond preoccupation with money and competition to developing a deeper meaning in life. Their spiritual growth was immensely important in their lives.

Also, they used the difficulties of their childhood to develop empathy for others. Empathic range was a predictor of optimal health in adulthood. In essence, these seemingly Type-A individuals are in actuality Type-E (empathy) achievers. We now have a new generalization to ponder!

The individuals in the Sound Mind-Sound Body study have proved that achievement, meaning, spiritual health and intimacy can all be attained when past hurts are resolved and a new self story is constructed. The following client stories will hopefully provide you with a context to consider the path to developing the ability to turn down the dial when needed.

Success Depends on Me

Paul is an entrepreneur currently in the middle of a major dilemma. His company needs major financing to bring a very interesting and possibly lucrative venture to fruition. He has been with this start-up for two years and has been unable to manage his anxiety and worry regarding the possible success or failure of his company.

He was referred to me by a friend whom I had treated some time ago for a similar problem. Paul has worn down his teeth from grinding at night and has become completely overwhelmed at times to the point that he will go into the office at one or two in the morning when he can't sleep.

Of course, the major investors love his undying commitment to his work. They also pressure him constantly to assure them of the value of their investment before they commit more money. He made an interesting analogy at one point to try to explain how he feels working with these investors: "Doc, it's like all-star pitching vs. all-star hitting. You just don't know who is going to win. It's on that level."

Paul is obviously a preoccupied man and is constantly "on." His wife describes him as "always somewhere else" and "constantly thinking about the next problem to be faced and conquered."

Through our meetings, changing his story and grounding that story in personal experience, he has gradually developed a more balanced lifestyle. He was so desperate to calm down that he told me to just direct him and he would follow my directives to a tee. "I can't do it anymore. I don't want to fail after all this time. I don't want to disappoint people who are counting on me and whom I have convinced that this is a worthwhile venture. I need to pull it off, but I'll never last living like this."

Managing Your Energy

The first step for Paul was the recommendation that he start exercising again at an intensity level that worked for him. After all, on top of all the demands he had, the one thing he didn't want to do is overexert himself. Yet exercising is a primary way to channel nervous energy into an outcome that benefits his body and whole way of being.

Paul had been a soccer player in high school, so he knew the benefits of exercise. When I informed him of the advantages in terms of reducing anxiety, he began the next day. He has been running the last several months and, of course, this has helped. The running has increased dopamine and nor-epinephrine in his brain, increasing his focus and allowing him to feel calm, even if for brief amounts of time.

I also told him that he needed to learn how to use empathy to immerse himself in the experiences of other people. This, too, was a lifestyle skill that took time for him to develop. Ironically he found this skill most helpful with his investors. Rather than just trying to assure and please them, he actually began listening to them on a deeper level.

He began to appreciate their concerns differently and in the process, realized they were not independently wealthy and were also worried. They were not feeling failed by him, but were also struggling with the same anxiety he had and some appreciated his understanding.

Others didn't care much about a relationship with Paul. They just wanted a return on their money. Empathy helped him to not personalize their responses. He realized they were in this for a particular purpose and their lack of interest in him was not a personal slight.

Over time, we worked on Paul taking vacations, which is an essential way to manage your energy. In fact, I was recently kidding with him that he's starting to take more time off than me. He once thought my taking three separate vacations a year was a bit excessive, but now he understands the importance.

He has also begun a different dialogue with his adolescent daughters. He is paying more attention to their words and, though difficult, he attends their plays and extracurricular activities without checking his email every so often.

His relationship with his wife has proven more trying. She has suffered through the years with his inability calming down. At one point last year, she told him she was not sure she still loved him. She told him she always felt tense around him. "You're either on or you're asleep. There is never anything in the middle. I can't ever relax in your presence, and I feel like a slacker when I'm relaxing and you're running around the house like a man with an incredibly important mission."

She went on to say that their friends have commented in the same regard. Even though Paul has improved, I am afraid his wife has seen the light in the dining room as too bright for too long. I don't know whether or not Paul will be able to save his marriage. I do know that he has begun to change in a way that has allowed him to calm himself. If he continues, it may manifest itself as a healing agent in his marriage.

Paul's life has been drastically changed. He has returned to exercise after a long hiatus and, as a result, has changed his neurochemistry, producing much needed, soothing chemicals. He has learned to listen from an empathic viewpoint. He has received feedback from colleagues and friends alike that they feel calmer in his presence. This is obviously what his wife wanted all along. Maybe, as she experiences this newfound ability, she will begin to believe in the positive possibilities of their marriage once more. In time…we will see.

The Calming Agent—Empathy

In order to calm yourself in a difficult situation, you have to be able to perceive accurately. This is where empathy is crucial. Paul had difficulty sleeping; he tossed and turned all night because he misperceived the outcome of his actions. He was so worried about how others would feel about him if the venture failed, but rarely checked out this concern with his colleagues. This is a primary example of a fictional story that we make up and yet continue to live with. Because of the lack of empathy in genuine relation with others, perception is not checked with reality.

On one occasion, he left a very important meeting in India, believing the associates he was meeting with were disappointed with him. He even allowed himself to think they were considering pulling out of the deal being negotiated.

After one of our sessions, where we turned the dial down and examined the potential consequences, he realized he was probably assuming far too much. He later sent an email to the associates and followed up with a phone call to discuss reactions to the meeting. He learned that his concerns were off-base. The individuals involved did say they had concerns, but over time their questions were answered and they decided to move forward.

Life is a Team Effort

One variable Paul had not considered (that continually fueled his inability to turn the dial down,) was his exaggerated sense of the consequences of his actions. He came to learn that he was taking on far too much responsibility for the decisions of others. I asked him once if he bought stock in a particular company on the advice of his broker and the stock lost money, would he call his broker and blame him for the outcome. He said he wouldn't, but he would be disappointed if it happened more times than not.

Of course he was referring to an average (the amount of times he would be misguided,) not making a decision to disengage from the broker for one ill-fated stock purchase. In addition, he realized there is a chance element in all these undertakings. If you think you're the only variable that counts in the outcome of a venture or, for that matter in any activity, you're going to have a very difficult time developing a dimmer switch.

One of my clients, a former professional athlete, would come to sessions and bemoan certain games he played when the team would lose and his performance was less than stellar. I had to remind him several times that he was part of a *team*. He was not the only variable. He was another individual who couldn't turn down the dial because he often misjudged the depth of responsibility he was accountable for.

The only way he could relax at night was to drink scotch. Eventually, the scotch brought him to me. He transferred his attitude from playing a sport to his work in the corporate world. He traded the athletic team for the corporate team. His inability to perceive accurately made him too edgy in both situations. After all, he was the nucleus of the team in both worlds, for better or worse.

Capable, driven people, especially those with PA, come to believe that their capabilities make them responsible for outcomes that are completely irrational. They have grown up, however, with this belief system being reinforced, especially when they have performed at levels that are admirable and bring other people joy (especially if their efforts bring joy to a parent's fragile ego.) The pattern becomes addictive.

If you're primarily recognized when you excel, not for your character (the essence of who you are,) the errant belief system takes hold. Thus my client saw himself as a loser when his team lost or his organization was failing. The pressure created a bright light in his brain that could not be dimmed and, unfortunately, alcohol abuse became the sole way of turning it off.

Healthy, high achieving people who have a dimmer switch have emotions that fit the situations they are in. They are in sync with their surroundings and their empathy allows them to perceive accurately. They have more flexibility in their personalities. They tear up at funerals and laugh heartedly at parties. They feel sad when the situation calls for sadness, and feel regret when they make a mistake.

When they make mistakes, however, or things do not go their way, they don't think they are a mistake as a person. They turn the dial down, know how to relax and realize that tomorrow brings a new opportunity for success. They essentially have a resilient sense of self.

The Dimmer Switch is about YOU, Not Your Environment

Interestingly, a conversation with one of my clients stuck with me in this regard. Alice is a 78-year-old woman who was a schoolteacher in her early years but left her profession to be with her two sons full-time. Her boys are married with children and doing well in most areas of their lives. Alice's husband died of a massive heart attack when she was in her early 50's and she remarried at age 64.

Her current husband, age 70, is remarkably healthy and quite active. Most days he is off golfing, skiing or playing tennis with friends. He is also quite involved with his grandkids, so he is often out doing things on his own. Alice married again because she could not stand living alone and because "I refuse to live in one of those public housing places for the elderly."

She is often trying to gain her husband's approval as he is far less-validating than her first spouse. She tries to redo curtains in the living room, feels compelled to plant more and more flowers around the house and tries hard to cook pleasing meals. These efforts are very similar to her trying to please her father in her youth. She was the oldest and only girl whose two younger brothers were given more leeway. In those days, the daughter was supposed to make sure the house was immaculate, since her mother worked full-time.

Alice said to me the other day, "We have talked about the dimmer switch in our sessions, and the thing that is amazing to me is I always thought I had a constant 'to do' list in my pocket because I was teaching or because I had young kids. But today and for the last several years, I still have that list with me all the time. I don't sleep any better. I am still an anxious person and I realize I have conditioned myself to be anxious, to always believe there is something unfinished, something or someone who needs my attention. My God, what would the world do without Alice? I'm coming to the end of my life and I am still acting like the little girl trying desperately to get Daddy to say, 'Great job Alice.' How very foolish I have been."

This interaction reaffirmed for me how powerful our conditioning can be to move faster, produce more and never slow down. For some, this is the only way they believe they can win love. Unfortunately for Alice, it has taken her whole life to come to this realization. Her mother lived to age 98 and I believe Alice can live the next 20 or so years in a state of peace she has never experienced before.

Why do I have such optimism? Because I can see in her eyes there is nothing she wants more. At her age, she drives an hour to see me each and every week with clear memory of what we discussed the week before.

Also, and most importantly, she is trying to make changes. She leaves the "to do" list on her kitchen table some days and goes for a short walk, then returns to her yard and forces herself to sit and enjoy looking at her garden rather then always focusing on improving the yard.

She has begun the process and I know she is committed to stopping the incessant demands of her own mind. She knows her story is more like a novel. It is inaccurate, and she is trying to create a more comfortable lifestyle based on new truths she is learning about herself.

Do You Know What's Driving You?

If you are having difficulty turning down the dial, your answers to the following questions should be revealing and informative. Your responses could give you the information needed to manage your energy effectively.

Questions to Journal:

- How often, during the course of a day, do you feel calm?

- Do you find it difficult to slow down enough to truly listen to another person? If so, why?

- Do you have difficulty with unstructured time?

- Do you have difficulty falling asleep or staying asleep?

- Do you have a "to do" list in your mind or in your pocket at all times?

- Do you take pride in accomplishing more than other people?

- Do you often tell people how many hours you have worked or how much you have accomplished in a day?

- Do you often feel like you work more than other people and others take advantage of you?

- Do you realize that your tendency to be intense is your own doing, or do you think it is due do to the inefficiency of others?

- Do you feel uncomfortable when you're not accomplishing or not achieving?

- Do you resent people who are not particularly impressed with your work ethic?

- Can you slow down and still feel worthy or are you afraid to lose your edge?

- Do you use alcohol or other substances to lessen your tension at night?

- Do you use comfort foods to excess at night to calm down?

- Do you watch TV or scan the internet to dull your anxiety in the evening?

- If you answered "yes" to any of the preceding ques tions, take a moment and explain your response.

Get Grounded in Experience

1. In an important conversation, try to slow down your rate of speech. Be conscious of your breathing and try to respond in a more thoughtful manner. Notice how empathic listening auto- matically turns down the dial.

2. Consider the personal and professional benefits of this approach and how it could affect your future positively.

Chapter 15:
Courage in the Midst of Fear—A Resilient Sense of Self

A person who possesses a resilient sense of self can most often cope effectively in the face of uncertainty. In the face of change, he/she has the required agility we all need to take care of ourselves and thrive in today's fast-paced world. Anxiety and fear, for example, can be managed without overwhelming emotions becoming dominant.

Healthy high achievers can address conflict successfully and with courage despite being scared or vulnerable.

Vulnerability and Courage—Unlikely Partners

At the time of this writing, Professor Randy Pausch, author of *The Last Lecture* and video of the same title, died a few days ago. Randy has influenced thousands of people around the world with his tremendous spirit for life and his courage in facing terminal pancreatic cancer.

The words in Randy's book are not exceptional in and of themselves, but nevertheless it is rated #1 on most book lists. I think the reason for his book's success is that people know the exceptional aspect of his life was his behavior and his resiliency in the face of mortality. His words were matched by the way he led his life. I recommend you read his book or watch the video of his last lecture. It will leave you with an emotional memory that will guide you toward living fully.

I have described a number of people throughout this book who have the kind of resiliency Professor Pausch possessed, but they will never write a book or appear on Oprah. They are extra ordinary people working and growing personally and, in the process, developing a resilient sense of self.

A person does not possess this kind of resiliency by accident. It is a learned attribute that develops as a result of your interactions in life. Randy Pausch gives many examples in his book of support, guidance and love from many sources. He behaved in an incredibly inspiring fashion. He was able to internalize the goodness he was given by others. He was able to believe in himself as others did and, most importantly, he was able to give back what he had received. Amazingly, even at the hour of his death, he was still giving inspiration to the thousands of cancer sufferers throughout the world.

We love these kinds of real life examples of resiliency, especially in the face of our most feared enemy—mortality. Another book, *Tuesday's With Morrie*—the story of another professor, Morrie Schwartz and his conversations with his former student Mitch Albom—is still inspiring many readers to this day.

We identify with the wish to be brave and strong at our most uncertain times in life. Ironically, I think the characteristics of Randy and Morrie are similar—vulnerability and courage experienced simultaneously.

The ability to give as one suffers and the ability to be strong when one is most insecure make individuals most appealing.

Why? Because these individuals are *real*!

We believe their experience to be true because they reveal their true nature. They are not pretending to be without fear. They are not superhuman. They are human beings at their realistic best. They are being the best they can be, given what they have to work with (in this case, a terminal illness.) You don't need a terminal illness to experience this resiliency.

Intelligent Optimism

If we look below the surface, what do Randy Pausch and Morrie

Schwartz have in common? A strong marriage, a love of life and a desire to impart all that they have learned to others.

They both had an ability to address fear head-on and knew when to let go of control. They had realistic expectations, an ability to be intimate and each possessed a community of friends. They had few regrets, as they lived life fully to the end. They had an unending passion for learning and growing, a love of exercise and using their bodies, a commitment to overall health, passion for life, an appreciation of the little things and a desire to impart all the knowledge they had about life to as many people as possible.

It is no surprise they were both professors. Professors are not known for being multi-millionaires, but they are known for having a profound influence on young minds. They are also known for acting younger than their chronological age.

We came to love them, these two men we never met face to face. Take a moment to reflect on that fact. They are loved and yet most people never met them. People will be reading their books long after they are gone and many future authors like me will be quoting them; Why?

I think you know the answer. They overcame a potentially unsupportive story around their present fate, resolved to not be controlled by the emotional trials and therefore steered clear of distorted thinking. **They were intimately familiar with each aspect of living free.**

Do you realistically think Randy or Morrie were not aware of the pitfalls of an unsupportive story or of comparing their situation and circumstances to others? How about buying in to the religion of perfection, pathological certainty, image love, etc.?

They certainly seemed to understand what arrogance can breed. They understood that, no matter how capable you are, you can be diagnosed with a life-ending illness. They had humility, even though they were accomplished in their fields.

Their writings and the words of their associates indicate they were intelligently optimistic. They were not simply die-hard pessimists or optimists, but realists. I have had many firsthand experiences with people who defy their history and life circumstances and develop amazing resiliency.

Overcoming *the Curse* with Resiliency

I have a client whose mother committed suicide when she was nine years old. Her mother came from a prestigious, New England family and "married down," according to her family. Mary's mother fell in love with a boy from lesser means.

Mary's mother had attended a private college, which was a rarity at the time. She was quite beautiful and meticulous about her appearance. She was struck by the physical appeal of her new, handsome boyfriend (Image Love.) Her infatuation dwindled as the years went on. Having children and being forced to go to work contributed to a feeling of being overwhelmed. None of her sisters had ever worked and all three had marriages of affluence that she envied.

The tension between her mother and her father was at a peak during Mary's childhood. Her mother constantly chided her husband for not being successful and not providing more for his family. He gradually retreated into a depressed, avoidance state of being. At the time of her death, Mary's mother was employed by one of the most successful men in her small town as his personal secretary.

Those are all facts my client Mary, age 62, gleaned over time about her mother. Some were from personal experience and some from aunts who became more open and revealing in the later years of their lives.

A few years after the loss of her mother, her father moved Mary and her older sister to Minnesota, a state of which he had no knowledge or history. He had acquired a new job because he felt this would give the family a fresh start. He wanted to live in a place where no one would ask questions about Mary's mother, a place where the past could be forgotten. Well, this plan didn't work.

He remarried a woman with two children of her own when Mary was twelve. His new wife and her family started to ask questions during their engagement. Eventually, he told all of them the truth.

Unfortunately, he was haunted by his wife's death, a suicide from an overdose of barbiturates. He eventually began drinking more and more until he became unable to work. He was admitted to a detox hospital but never got sober thereafter for very long.

Eventually, Mary's aunt brought her back to Massachusetts and raised her along with her own two sons. Mary was with her aunt from the age of thirteen until she finished high school. Although her aunt, a widow, focused more on her biological children, she helped Mary develop a very deep spiritual life that Mary credits with giving her solace in her darkest moments.

After leaving her aunt's house and moving in with a friend who worked at the same insurance agency, Mary met her future husband and married him within the year. They soon had a son and daughter. Mary cherished being a mother.

Sadly, over the years it became apparent that her husband was an alcoholic. Mary didn't understand that he was suffering from alcoholism for some time. But eventually and painfully, she realized the magnitude of the problem.

When her children were ten and twelve, her husband had an affair with a very close friend of Mary's and eventually left her. They divorced and he married her friend several years later. Also around this time both her adult children had become alcoholic, which caused even more pain. She was devastated and sought therapy, but after eight months of counseling, her therapist moved to California.

The Beginning of Freedom

Mary worked at a local hospital as an administrative assistant. A friend in the admitting office gave her my name. Upon meeting Mary, I could see how guarded she was. At the same time, I could sense how much she wanted to be helped.

Mary asked several interesting questions: "Will you be staying in this area for a long time or might you be moving at some point?" Have you worked with women or mostly men? Do you have a wife and children? How many years have you been married? How many hours do you work? Will you have a regular time for me? Are you experienced treating people with addictions? Have you experienced any losses in your life?"

Most people in an initial interview will ask one or two questions and many say they have nothing to ask when I inquire.

Mary knew exactly what she was looking for, she'd had enough disappointment in her life and only wanted to work with a psychologist who had the qualities and experience she knew she needed.

The questions she asked were all focused on the major hurts in her life. She desperately wanted to know if I was the person who could help her with these momentous events she had lived through. Even though she was suffering, she was unusually focused and determined. I thought, in those initial moments, that her determination and courage would be her saving grace.

Mary was all about consistency and dependability. She began our initial individual sessions in a purposeful manner. She had much to talk about and she came with an agenda every week. I could also see how she was assessing whether or not she could trust me.

She examined all nuances of my behavior and was very sensitive to any change in my demeanor, the time we met or any indication of a future change. She was clearly on the lookout for additional disappointment in her life and she tried to be prepared to prevent a fall into the deep depression of her past.

We began meeting in the summer. When I announced I was taking a vacation in a few months, she was markedly affected. She associated my leaving with all the losses in her life and acknowledged at one point that she was fearful something would happen to me.

On another occasion, I changed offices in the hospital where I was working. It took her several weeks to feel comfortable in the new setting. Clearly, anytime change was in the making, she felt a loss of security. She had an expectation that change meant emotional pain was around the corner. Considering her background, this was certainly understandable.

The Power of the Group

Mary eventually joined one of my group sessions with much trepidation. She found it very difficult to trust members with her private thoughts and frequently held back what she really felt about other people.

She chose to remain silent or to talk about her history in a way that kept others from commenting. She would reveal an aspect of her life, her mother's suicide for instance, and then reach a conclusion as to how that tragedy was affecting her. She implied that there was no need for any further exploration before anyone else could render a comment.

Over time she came to realize she was protecting herself from feedback she thought could be hurtful by using this style. Mary also had an unusually hard time when a new member would join the group. She again assumed this was another person capable of hurting her, so she would retreat into a cautious position.

Weeks and months passed. Slowly Mary became more and more attached to group members. She was particularly connected to a few members who were recovering alcoholics and to one executive, an Ivy League grad, who had made a suicide attempt. She was quite surprised that such accomplished people could feel so dissatisfied with their lives. Ultimately she came to understand that this was the same curiosity she had about her accomplished mother.

Unconsciously Mary had expected the women in the group to be like her mother, someone she really never got to know but left her feeling devastated. She expected the men to be unreliable, unfaithful and overall not worth getting involved with.

Ironically, this group was made up of people who are all high achievers and Mary initially thought she had little to give them. They came to view her as steadfast and salt of the earth. They loved her practical approach to life and encouraged her feedback. She seemed to understand the strife in their lives unlike most people.

Once she began to trust people, she was free to demonstrate her tremendous capacity to be empathic. She knew what it felt like to suffer. She understood the experience of severe anxiety and how tension can dominate someone's very existence. She started to see that she, the only non-college graduate in the group, had much to give these bright, educated people. Her sense of self was beginning to blossom in a way that she seldom experienced.

Mary grew up not really knowing much about her mother or father, never having the opportunities to be close to them. She was curious about what made people do destructive things.

Mary received much help from the recovering alcoholics in the group in learning how to help her children's drinking problem. While in group, her son received his first and second DUI. She eventually, with the expert guidance of the group, got him into AA and after several setbacks, he eventually became sober.

Her son has now been sober for six years. The same process took place with her daughter. With the oldest child already in sobriety, Mary employed the same structure for her youngest and joined AA herself. She is still an active member of AA today and, sponsors several women in that program currently.

Through the group, Mary began to trust more and more and today is a far more relaxed person who smiles often, unlike before. She still lives alone, but takes great pride in watching her grandchildren since both her son and daughter are married and living in the area.

She is a very spiritual woman and is very involved in her church. She would tell you her faith in God kept her coming to therapy as she prayed on a daily basis for God to help her live a more balanced life.

As Mary's confidence in herself grew, her fear of others lessened. Over time she became much more welcoming to new members and is not nearly as afraid of new situations. She has learned that her suffering has given her the ability to understand people on a very deep level, a quality that is valued by many.

One of the men in group told Mary that he somehow missed getting "the empathy chip" when he was born. He believed she surgically planted it in his brain through her way of being with him; thus the positive effect of the 6th trial—community.

Overcoming Painful History

As Mary's self esteem improved, she was also more able to talk about the past. She always wondered why a person would take his or her own life. She longed to have a glimpse into her mother's heart. She eventually started to visit more relatives and asked many questions about her mother.

Mary found out her mother took her life one week after her boss was killed in a car accident. Her aunt speculated that Mary's mother was involved with her boss in a love relationship. There was even speculation that Mary's sister was not her own father's biological child. This news, whether correct or not, troubled Mary to the point that she fell into a depression for a brief time.

Mary started to drink at night to soothe the pain. The information made her feel like she didn't belong anywhere. I remember her saying, "The more I learn, the stranger I feel. I just don't belong anywhere. These people tell me stories about my family that seem unreal, like I was never part of that world they lived in."

The understanding Mary received when she returned to group with this news about family brought her to tears. Other people in group talked of not really knowing their family members. One woman commented that she knew Mary much more than her own two sisters.

Another man stated that his parents never communicated about anything of substance, but stuck to clichés he had heard a million times and never seemed to want to delve beyond the surface.

Mary was not alone. She received empathy that eventually healed the wounds of her lost childhood. She stopped drinking during this time and never resumed. She was never able to give up smoking, and although she has reduced the amount, this habit that started at age fourteen still has a hold on her.

I will always remember one group when she was asked what she would do if she could see her mother one last time. "What would you ask her? What do you still want to know?"

Mary's answer was, "All I want is to hug her and have her hold me. I don't have any questions. The facts don't seem very important anymore, but the chance to hold her would mean the world to me."

Over time, Mary has let go of most of the curiosity that used to plague her. She certainly still wonders, but not in a disturbing way. It's no longer a necessity to have the facts. Her answer to the question posed indicated she just wanted the warmth and affection of a mother she never knew. She strongly sensed how it would feel to hug her once again. She returned to the warmth and let go of the strife.

Mary likes to quote an AA saying, "Let Go and Let God," and I think it is her way of acknowledging that we can move ahead without knowing why people hurt us. We can't always have all those answers. Her healing took place without the facts but with love, compassion, empathy and understanding, a relational healing.

Today Mary is retired, quite active in her community, in her church, in AA and as a grandparent. She also belongs to a reading group, loves to garden and is living a meaningful life. She guided her adult children to sobriety and they are good parents and spouses.

Not surprisingly, her son is an addiction counselor at a hospital in nearby New Hampshire. Her daughter returned to graduate school to be a social worker after several years in the corporate world. I think they have Mary's heart and her willingness to give to others.

An Imperfect, Lovely Ending

Mary will probably never write a book or be on Oprah, but in my estimation, and in the minds of many who know her, she is a very high achiever. She, like Morrie and Randy, has developed a resilient sense of self in the face of enormous uncertainty and emotional pain.

It's ironic that Mary was the first to recommend I read *Tuesdays with Morrie*. She has also told me how very affected she has been to hear of Randy Pausch's death. She valued their stories as they are so resonate to her own.

Mary doesn't live a perfect life today according to her hopes and dreams.

She had always secretly wished she would meet a man and remarry, but it just didn't work out that way; at least not yet. She has always had difficulty maintaining an exercise program, but has started walking at least a few times a week. Her cigarette habit is one that still gnaws at her but one she eventually may conquer.

Nevertheless, Mary is a success story by all accounts! "Friday's with Mary" have been quite an experience for all of us in the group. Her growth has made us all a bit more resilient!

Life Situations are Random, but Resiliency is a Choice

Writing a self-help book is quite difficult in that authors have to appeal to a wide range of readers, be succinct in our message and reveal unique insights that are not simply rehashing much of what has already been written. It seems like Norman Vincent Peale's book *The Power of Positive Thinking* is rewritten every year with several new titles.

I am an avid reader of journals, texts and articles that relate to well-being in the areas of nutrition, spirituality, exercise and, of course, psychology. My clients and associates frequently send me articles, books and internet sites that cover these areas. I try valiantly (although not always successfully) to read and integrate as much as I can in my life and in my work.

In the last year I have read two self-help books that I would highly recommend as they relate directly to the topic of resiliency and overall health. They are also atypical in that they are based on solid research and describe two major factors central to successfully "healing" *the curse*: 1) The acceptance of our inability to predict the future and the fact that situational variables will alter our lives (control) and 2) The realization that we can learn to be happy and resilient, despite our genetic makeup and history, based on improving our ability to perceive accurately (empathy).

Professor Dan Gilbert's book *Stumbling on Happiness* is full of contemporary research that is rendered to the reader in a flowing, humorous style that is easy to comprehend. He establishes one salient point that is central to our agenda: human beings have illusions of foresight.

We think we can predict the future and the direction of our lives, but we are quite inept in forecasting the paths our lives will take. When you look back over the past five or ten years, haven't there been several key events in your life you would have never predicted?

When we give up the inordinate need for control, we can essentially "stumble on happiness."

Human beings have an extreme desire for control. When we are unable to control our future (if it doesn't materialize as we expect,) we can become quite unhappy and distressed. Driven high achievers, those suffering from PA in particular, have a very difficult time believing that their efforts will not be able to move the future in the direction they prefer.

As you have seen with several of my clients, they do not factor in the situational variables in life, holding themselves responsible for events that are clearly out of their control. Perfectionism does not allow for the reality that we often lack control outside of ourselves.

Mary has developed a resilient sense of self because she accepts the twists and turns in life. She is not responsible for her mother's suicide or her children's alcoholism. As the old saying goes, "Stuff happens." Mary and all of my clients, who have succeeded in conquering the curse, have come to accept that control of the future is futile.

We can do all we can to take care of ourselves and those around us, but the longing to have certainty in an uncertain future has to be relinquished to feel comfortable in your own skin. Resilience is intimately associated with acceptance of the situational variables in life and, of course, resiliency is fostered when we have faith in ourselves to cope with whatever comes our way.

Dr. Stefan Klein is a science writer in Berlin, Germany, who is well-known throughout Europe for his expertise in brain research as it pertains to happiness and resiliency. His acclaimed book *The Science of Happiness* details the latest discoveries in neuroscience and psychology that explain how we can maintain happiness and develop a solid sense of self.

One major finding pertinent to our quest is the fact that **happiness is dependent on the way the brain perceives, not on the environment we encounter**. Dr. Klein is essentially describing the capacity for empathy—the accurate reading of the people and circumstances in our lives. Happiness then becomes a state of mind that can be learned as empathy can be learned.

Interestingly, Klein describes addiction as an "accident that happens in the course of the human search for happiness."

We are all on a quest for happiness and addictions like PA and others are side streets we go down in a desperate attempt to stimulate dopamine, the neurochemical chiefly responsible for happiness. In addicted behavior our desire is out of control since some individuals have lost or never had the ability to establish a happy lifestyle naturally.

Dopamine is produced through addictive behavior which is not conducive to building a solid sense of self. In fact, it creates more and more doubt in your faith to produce a lifestyle of happiness and meaning.

Klein emphasizes that learning is a natural experience that makes people happy and that the brain runs on fun (dopamine.) The sensation of pleasure is produced in discovery (hopefully, you are having such an experience at this moment in your exploration throughout this book.)

Large European studies confirmed that searching for fame, money and good looks leads to dissatisfaction. However those people who develop their potential, have good relationships and are active in social causes have higher rates of happiness. They are more secure and, in the process, they protect the health of their brains and their neurological system.

As you come to understand and begin to remove the factors that distort thinking; after gaining perspective on the six trials of adult life, examine the role of PA in your life and the novel that contributed to its existence, you have finally arrived at the juncture which provides the foundation for a resilient sense of self!

Questions to Journal:

- Do you consider yourself a resilient person?

- If not, what are the key areas where you are stuck?

- Do you believe you have understood the significance of the six trials?

- Which of the trials is preventing you from being resilient?

- How can you address those trials differently for success?

- Can you allow yourself to be vulnerable without feeling inadequate?

- If not, what is the nature of your thinking that interferes?

- Do you participate in any group experiences, either informal or formal, that provide feedback to you about your personality?

- If not, what are the reasons you avoid group opinions?

- When is the last time you encountered a difficult conflict? How did you cope?

- What do you think you need to change about yourself in order to feel more at ease with yourself?

- Lastly, what are the ingredients you consider important for establishing resiliency? What is your own unique perspective?

Get Grounded in Experience

1. In a conversation with someone you trust, try to reveal a recent fear you experienced and discuss a way of dealing with this fear constructively. Ask his or her opinion and have a give-and-take conversation. Ask your friend if he or she has observed this reaction of fear in you before. Ask what he or she would consider a resilient reaction given the situation you described.

2. Determine what has been missing in your attempts to develop resiliency from the feedback you received. Record which ways of thinking detract from resiliency and ask for the help of others in developing a more optimistic way of perceiving.

Chapter 16:
With an Open Heart and Open Mind—The Spiritual Learner

Before you assume this chapter is about religion in the formal sense, please be patient and read the following story.

The other day one of my group clients who understands *the curse* as well as anyone told us of a very interesting interaction he had with his oldest son.

Antonio is a handsome, articulate corporate executive who was a star soccer player in high school and in college. He has a successful marriage and is a committed father to his son and daughter. His resume has always been exceptional but nevertheless Antonio grew up with his heart marred by *the curse*. The reasons were hidden that continually left him feeling "less than" despite his achievements. Over time he has re-written his story and is emerging with a new more positive view of himself based on his character rather than exclusively on his performance.

His oldest son, now 12, continually asks him why he goes to group meetings every Friday morning, "What does that "Semisola" (that's how he pronounced my last name) guy do for you that makes you want to go back?" he'd ask his father.

Antonio had been feeling a bit shameful about attending sessions as his oldest had been chiding him recently, implying he was not working out things on his own. Even though he tried to explain, he couldn't quite make his eldest son understand that "group" was not an activity to be embarrassed about.

On one particular day when his son persisted in questioning him, he felt caught in a bit of a dilemma. He just responded spontaneously and said "he is my spiritual advisor." Young Tony was, for the moment, satisfied and the discussion ended.

Antonio was surprised that this description appeased his son. His wife was standing in the kitchen, listening and smiling, "You sure dodged a bullet this time," and they laughed together.

Ironically, when Antonio was relating this story in group he confessed, "Although it seemed funny at the time, in retrospect it rings true. When I leave group I almost always feel my spirits have been lifted. It's not so much a religious thing, but I do feel something good is released in me. We often talk of spiritual learning and I think it means opening yourself up in ways you never have before. You're the guide in this process Dr. C., so I guess somewhere inside me I had designated you as my spiritual advisor".

He asked me what I thought the term meant, "Spiritual advisor." I also responded spontaneously, "I think it is when one person enlivens the spirit of another, when new learning and new growth are stimulated and it leaves a person with a feeling of excitement and energy."

I decided to include a chapter on *Spiritual Learning* after hearing this story as I have referred to the term throughout this book. I think it is necessary to further clarify its meaning. I also know, through experience with many who struggle with *the curse*, that the end result of their work is often symbolized by becoming spiritual learners. It is a clear indication that distorted thinking has been abandoned and new, more accurate thinking has taken its place.

What is a *Spiritual Learner*?

The spiritual learner is someone who realizes there is something beyond ourselves that influences and accounts for life events—an intangible that cannot completely be explained. For many this is the work of God, for others it is the work of the "Universe;" and for others it is simply an undefined spiritual experience.

A spiritual learner is a person who takes in information from diverse sources. In terms of religion, he or she is a person who realizes and accepts that all the major religions have made worthwhile contributions. A spiritual learner is an open-minded person who expects to continue to gain wisdom about the human condition throughout life. He or she expects to revise theories and change perspective as new learning takes place. He or she may or may not be wedded to one way of thinking, one psychology or one religious orientation. This is important to living a balanced, healthy, high-achieving life because we are constantly faced with new situations that require that we adapt and change.

The perspective of being a spiritual learner can be applied to most aspects of life. Any fixed way of thinking and behaving that has rendered an unhealthy outcome should be reevaluated. Individuals of this persuasion are not threatened to reconsider behavioral patterns that have become entrenched but may need adjusting, or may need to be totally abandoned.

In my family, for instance, the men were all heavy smokers. It seemed like the thing to do and it seemed perfectly healthy for the World War II generation. It was endorsed at the time by many doctors and scientists who were paid by the tobacco industry.

As a young child I pleaded with my father to stop smoking but it was to no avail. I could hear him cough every morning. It just didn't seem like it was good for him but I had no data to support my argument. Ultimately the habit that gave him comfort in World War II took his life at age 66.

My father was just beginning to turn the corner in his thinking. Of course his severe addiction altered his intention on most occasions. The day he died he was down from four packs of Chesterfields a day to four cigarettes. He was beginning to employ a spiritual learner perspective to his addiction when time ran out. He was entertaining the possibility that his belief about the innocence of smoking was wrong and he was starting to consider an alternate outlook. He realized that his behavior was robbing his spirit of energy (he was sick more often, had shortness of breath as his body was failing him and his spirit for life was diminishing) and he was trying valiantly to change his beliefs and behavior.

Learning Connects Us

In this regard I believe that part of the appeal of Tibetan Buddhism for Americans is the ongoing efforts of the Dali Lama to learn and integrate new findings. The Dali Lama has often stated that Buddhism is an ancient religion with many ancient texts. Yet he has indicated that the teaching of these texts needs to change according to new knowledge. He has displayed openness to scientific knowledge, particularly the neuroplasicity (thinking and experience changes brain structure) of the brain.

This kind of orientation to life makes our days more interesting, increases energy and allows us to be part of a wider world. We are more connected to an array of individuals and experiences. Spiritual learners are invested in discovering and experiencing whatever enlivens the human spirit in a healthy way.

Being a spiritual learner naturally gives us the tools to rewrite our story. Remember part of the definition is "to learn from all credible sources," including ourselves. This means we now have an opportunity to take in accurate information about ourselves, our beliefs, our career paths and most importantly, our culture, country and world.

We cannot live free of *the curse* if we are not concerned with people throughout the world. Personal liberation requires an awareness of the fact that certain societies, cultures and organizations create systems that enslave others. If we are self-absorbed and just tend to those closest to us who are most like us, we create a small non-diverse world which limits our personal and spiritual growth. **In essence, the well-being of others is our well-being.**

There is no separation for the spiritual learner. Our story can now be rewritten because we trust the opinions of others, and in a global sense we trust that those around the world have important insights and wisdom to contribute.

A Life of Truth

Spiritual learners rewrite their unsupportive story in on-going fashion. They have developed hope and trust in others and have come to realize that self-learning and learning about the world is endless. It is exciting to have this philosophy in your heart as learning no longer becomes threatening, but rather becomes a constant way of enhancing your sense of self.

You become liberated, open to all those around you and, most importantly, you are opening to the world at large. You now are a contributor to a better society because you are free to be a genuine participant. No more cover ups, no more need to protect a false story.

The greatest feeling is to know the old story is mostly made-up.

Rewriting our story is never just about our rearranging our internal view of ourselves. It is also about rearranging all we have learned that is inaccurate. For instance, baby boomers in the United States grew up believing German and Japanese people were evil and despicable. Turns out they thought the same of us and the propaganda of all three countries turns out to be false.

Today, many young people are growing up thinking Muslims are violent, despicable, evil people. Some Americans pull Muslims out of their cars and beat them. What a horrible travesty; a misinformed manner of promoting violence and maintaining an unsupportive story of ourselves and many others, cutting off the opportunity for empathic understanding and vital connections. Remember that any distortion of the truth, in us or with others, can lead to self and societal destruction.

Spiritual learners are committed to the truth about themselves, their families, friends and all those who inhabit our world. We are committed to examining every bias in our minds and hearts so that we live in harmony with the truth.

If we are in opposition to the truth for fear and other defensive reasons, we are much more prone to developing and maintaining *the curse*. Why? Because, we are then constantly misdirected in terms of how to feel comfortable within ourselves and in the world; we are always hiding behind mythical beliefs about ourselves and others.

Freedom to Doubt

It is not necessary to be religious to be a spiritual learner. However, many people who are interested in their spiritual development have explored the major religions to ascertain their value.

Before I started writing about the six emotional trials of adulthood I re-read the classic *Religions of Man* by Huston Smith. It occurred to me over and over again, as I read through this wonderful book, how much people are missing who refuse to look beyond the religion of their childhood.

In the early years of my career, I consulted to the chaplaincy service in a local community hospital where I worked. I was fascinated to listen to the discussions between the hospital rabbi, minister and priest.

One Friday afternoon, I was sipping coffee with Rev. Dick Fleck, a Dominican priest and recovering alcoholic who has devoted years to working with alcoholic men and women. At age 75, he lives in a nursing home and still conducts AA meetings on Sunday nights in his residence. On this particular Friday I was a bit hesitant to ask but I got up the courage to remark that I wasn't always sure about the afterlife and my conception of God. Dick replied, "Join the club kid, we all feel that way at times."

I couldn't believe he also had doubts and he could see my surprise. "Without doubt you are just following blindly; true faith comes from the depths of doubt." His comments set me free and I was able to pursue spiritual and religious knowledge with an openness I hadn't previously experienced.

"My God, my God, why have you forsaken me?" are reportedly the last words of Jesus before He died. For the spiritual learner, faith will temporarily waiver internally and we will doubt whatever we believe in outside of ourselves.

But ultimately, freedom comes when we have the ability to maintain faith in ourselves and integrity in our behavior in the face of uncertainty and change. We vacillate and we all have doubts at times. Ultimately, through persistence we regain our perspective and we continue moving forward with new possibilities in sight. This is the life course of the spiritual learner.

The Spiritual Atheist

My atheist clients often assume that spiritual means something religious and they are turned off immediately. I recently defined spirituality to one of my clients who has an enormous disdain for formal religion. He has often said that "religion is the work of the right hemisphere making a great sale to the left." He pressed me one night to define *spiritual* as he was irritated by the constant use of the word in the recent Presidential primaries.

I answered, "Spiritual in its simplest form is the belief in the spirit of human beings, that intangible aspect of us that isn't entirely explainable and yet it is growth promoting."

When I defined spiritual learner he said I was describing him. **Spiritual people seek further knowledge and wisdom without bias and preconceived notions.** He was sitting in the chair before me with the same view but was immediately put off by the word (spiritual) before we explored its meaning. He expected some affiliation to a particular religion with accompanying religious dogma.

Theologian Karen Armstrong, a former Catholic nun from Ireland has written books on Judaism, Christianity, Islam and Buddhism. She was given the prestigious TED (Technology Entertainment Design) prize for her interfaith initiative called the "Charter of Compassion," bringing Muslim, Jewish, and Christian leaders in the world together to foster global understanding.

Interestingly, she states that compassion and empathy have been at the heart of all the major religious traditions. Most important in terms of understanding the Spiritual Learner is her contention that the great teachings had little to do with religion and religiosity. There was little interest in doctrine and being right and far more interest in fostering change through "human-heartedness."

I've Lost My Spirit

Loss of spirit usually is accompanied by depression, low mood and anxiety which correspond with low energy. We tend to over think when we have lost our spirit and sense of aliveness.

Eastern philosophies encourage people to move away from thought and into their senses, seeing thought as a potential contaminant to true understanding. This can be true, as we can ignore our emotions by thinking ourselves into a different state of mind.

Sadness, for instance, can be a guiding emotion. It slows our thinking and makes us more reflective if we allow this process to take place. If not, we convince ourselves through our thinking that sadness will make us weak. As a result we avoid and run past the important information our body is trying to give us.

When our personalities are resilient, we pay attention to our thoughts, emotions and energy levels without running. We can then determine which aspects of our lives may need more attention. Of course, this works both ways, meaning we can use an emotional cue to begin a negative cycle just as we can use an emotional cue constructively.

Sadness, regret, guilt, etc. can be guides to an aspect of the past that needs to be reviewed further. However, when we use emotional cues to start an obsessive negative thought process, we should de-invest rather than let our thoughts produce a low mood. An emotional cue is simply an aid, not a mechanism to start a repetitive whirlwind of despair. When people don't have the confidence in their ability to use emotion in a constructive manner, they rely on thought to guide them exclusively. This pattern can be quite limiting.

Freedom from the Challenges

We cannot obtain freedom from the challenges, and I do believe these are challenges all adults must face, if we are not open to new experiences and new ways of looking at ourselves and those in our lives. **Successfully working through the challenges requires we move past our fixed ideas of how to develop and maintain a balanced, healthy life.**

We don't maintain balance alone. It must be through the insights we gain as we are in relation to others. The human spirit longs for connection. Empathy provides the power to create intimate bonds with others.

In order to successfully maneuver through the challenges, we must be open to changing our thinking regarding the dysfunctional patterns discussed in this section. Lifting the barriers to empathy gives us the rich opportunity to learn from the wisdom of others, and as we give up our need to perfect ourselves, we are more likely to find real love.

With this foundation we are more apt to maintain our overall health, putting us in a position to learn about ourselves and others. We will always have differences with those close to us. But when we disagree with empathy we don't isolate ourselves, we remain in contact. We build our sense of self in the process by expanding our interpersonal skills. We open the door to the heart of another and in the process we increase understanding and are more likely to reach healthy compromises.

Concentration and Engagement

Spiritual learners tend to be focused; they have the ability to concentrate for a sustained period of time. Thus they are more available for relating and for the process of acquiring increased wisdom.

Spiritual learners, because they believe they can learn from people of many different persuasions, are more easily engaged. They don't dismiss the input of others quickly. They look for the nugget of truth in conversations and because they are looking and believing that nugget exists, they more often find pearls of wisdom.

Relational engagement, concentration and perceptual accuracy all make for utilizing our brains and hearts to their full capacity. Time stands still when we are fully present.

Achieving Without Worry

The life of a spiritual learner is a relational life, a belief in the power of others to increase each other's knowledge and enliven each other's heart. Of course, in order for this process to take place you must attain a comfort level with being vulnerable, with not being all-knowing but rather being in relationships to listen, learn and love.

In order to learn as much as possible from others empathy has to be expanded so that you can hear from a position that Quaker author Douglas Steers calls "Holy Listening—to listen another's soul into life, into a condition of disclosure and discovery." This kind of attentive, emphatic listening brings forth the deepest communication human beings can experience. It is truly a gift of spirit to both parties.

Having this perspective makes life so much easier. Our expectations are in order and we see each day as an opportunity for more enrichment. I don't mean this in an ideal sense. We all have good and bad days. I am talking about the fact that, when you are interested in learning for the right reasons, life becomes more bearable. The worry about aging, money and the future seems to occupy less of your thinking because you are engaged and enjoying your days for the most part.

Impediments to accomplishing or achieving are seen for what they are, opportunities to learn and grow. I think this type of individual builds skills in an easier fashion than most people because he or she is more comfortable with being in a learning process. This type of person tends to have a very accurate sense of a realistic learning curve given the situation.

Spiritual learners are certainly not suffering from pathological certainty. They have tolerance for being in a process, and thus have a dimmer switch. This allows them to be relatively calm in a learning process rather than worrying about how they are performing and how they are being viewed. They are not preoccupied with perfectionism and image, but rather are enjoying new learning and those they are encountering in the process. Learning makes them happy and it strengthens their physiology in the process.

Spiritual people tend to have more gratitude in life. They are more appreciative of what many often view as the "simple things." In a Buddhist sense, they slow down enough to smell, see and touch what many pass by and hardly notice. **They are excited about the life they are liv-**

**ing as opposed to be excited temporarily by the life they might have
if they achieve more or look better.**

Recently, when a friend asked me why I was writing another book,
my answer was, "Because I read the last one." She immediately thought
I was being critical of myself, but in fact, I was not. I was simply trying to convey that my last book was written in 2004. I have additional
wisdom and learning to impart five years later. At this point in my life, I
can't imagine a "last book," not as long as I am engaged, adding to my
knowledge base and integrating new ideas.

Learning about yourself and about human nature in general can only
help you cope more successfully in various stressful situations. As we
improve our relational abilities, lessen our tendencies to think irratio-
nally and improve our reading of others, we gain more and more ability
to   react with clarity and compassion.

The likelihood of this kind of growth becoming an ongoing part
of your life is directly correlated to your ability to learn from various
sources. We need to continually adjust to our ever-changing world.

Being a proactive learner means ongoing adjustment. Being a spiritual learner means ongoing adjustments based on ascertaining the truth
about ourselves, our environment and what it actually takes to thrive.

Questions to Journal:

- What does the word "Spiritual" mean to you?

- Do you struggle with formal religious concepts? If so, Why?

- Do you think spiritual development must be linked to a particular religion? If so, why?

- What in your life lifts your spirits consistently? Explain.

- What in your life deflates your spirit consistently? Explain.

- Do you maintain a childish view of religion or have you allowed yourself to express and work through your doubts?

- What are your doubts about religion?

- Do these questions interfere with your ongoing spiritual development? If so why?

- What aspects of being a Spiritual Learner do you find difficult to maintain?

- What aspects do you wish you could maintain?

- Does the level of openness of the Spiritual Learner scare you in any way?

- If so, why?

- What plan do you have to overcome your difficulty?

- Do you think you are a Spiritual Learner?

- Which aspects do you find easy to implement?

Get Grounded in Experience:

1. Describe the concept of the "Spiritual Learner" to two or more people close to you. Ask them what behaviors or ways of thinking you would need to improve to fit the definition. Find a way to experiment with implementing those changes in your current life.

2. Examine influential religious beliefs you grew up with, if any. Ask someone of a different religious background if they make rational sense and try to be open to his or her perspective.

Chapter 17:
Final Thoughts

As I have indicated throughout this book, living an energy-rich and satisfying life unencumbered by aspects of your past is a process.

The entire premise of the "hidden challenges" is an unsupportive story born primarily of a lack of empathy in genuine relationships with others and the resulting self-doubt and insecurity that emerges over time. This often gets covered up by unhealthy, if not addictive, behavior not the least of which is achievement.

In this book I highlight "Performance Addiction" where higher and greater achievement is thought to bring love and respect. Because love and respect are not found or defined solely by what you achieve, this compulsion leads to heightened emotional trials and distortions in thinking that make life difficult and well-being a forgotten state.

The Key to Freedom

We can never be completely free of any of life's trials. We can, however, develop the coping mechanisms necessary to address any and all challenges with confidence and stability; the most important of all is the ability to recognize the story(s) of your life that you tell each day. This is what drives your life experience.

The beauty of changing your story is that it can change your outdated beliefs, perspectives and the inaccuracies from your past. Changing your story allows you to purge the ones that are no longer serving you; your capabilities, achievements and your tendency to over-do have likely become a way of masking a fragile sense-of-self.

Your early story has profoundly influenced your view of yourself and the way you live your life. Hopefully you now realize your story was, at least in part, based on fiction. In order to re-write this early view of your-self, you have to discover a better view of who you really are and this happens best when you are in relationships with others who are giving you reasonable, objective feedback.

Finding this truth will truly liberate your soul. If you are doing and achieving for the right reasons, you will realize your potential. But if you're achieving for the wrong reasons (a futile attempt to change your internal view of yourself,) you become and will stay addicted to *the curse*.

The Stories That Moved You Are About You

As you reflect back on what you just read as well as your journal entries, you will probably remember certain stories that touched you deeper than others.

Did the story of Anthony's drive to perform move you? Or did Sara's obsession with Amazon evoke feelings in you as her inability to set real-istic expectations drove her downward? Did the stories of regret control and fear; the loss of a child, paralysis or the poignant stories of love lost and love regained move you? How about the two stories of dying men ending their lives quite differently in the community chapter?

Wherever you experienced strong emotion is where the bulk of your work lies. When emotion arises it generally means your past is being evoked.

It's worth repeating, I do not believe in belaboring the past, but I do believe your emotions will tell you where the past is interfering with the present. Those places are where you want to spend your time.

Journaling will be important in your ongoing growth. Your answers to the questions at the end of each chapter are important to re-visit now that you're finished reading this book.

I know, in the deepest part of my heart, that engaging in this process can change the quality of your life. I know it works because it's based on the actual experience of many people who have broken *"the curse."*

As I have said, I have been witness to the most amazing personal changes in the lives of achievers formally limited by *the curse*. I know that you can join the growing group of balanced, healthy high achievers, if you take the time and do the work.

Signs of Progression

I am often asked in my practice how a person will know if they are making progress changing their internal self view as indicated by new constructive behavior. A brief example of one person's unique journey is indicative of how a new story is born.

Remember Ruth from chapter 4 (Regrets and Unfulfilled Dreams)? She was called "Fatty" by her brothers and father. You may recall she, in desperation, had cosmetic surgery that went wrong. Breast implants became infected, leaving her with sagging breasts that added to her self hatred.

Well, last week in group, this formally inhibited woman told us of a change she made that really brought her incredible joy. She had been feeling despondent about the fact that she and her husband seldom make love, all the while knowing it was her anxiety about her body image that was interfering.

She got mad at herself, took a shower, combed her wet hair straight back and wrapped a towel around her waist. She went out into the room where Ray was watching TV and said, "I love you, I miss you and I want to make love now. And another thing, if you blow this I will kill you."

Of course we all laughed as Ruth went on to tell us that this sexual experience was phenomenal, "the best of my life." Ruth is certainly on her way to re-writing her story. She, in those moments, let go of her life-long story that, if you're not beautiful and providing for people at a very high level, they won't love you.

She had the courage to expose her imperfections and see if her old story really held true. It did not! She is desired as she is. We in group marveled at her ability to take a chance to once again find out the truth, rather than holding on to past perceptions that have paralyzed her ability to grow and make connections with others.

In group she has learned how to establish real intimacy and real friendship through honest, direct, tactful dialogue. At home she extended her learning to the physical realm. Ironically, we had just spent two consecutive sessions talking about the intimacy of kissing.

Several of the driven achievers in group admitted to seldom taking the time to "really kiss" their lovers or spouses, (passionate kissing releases the neurochemical oxytocin, which induces a feeling of trust and attachment) even though they all longed for greater intimacy. These verbal discussions about physical intimacy led to several members going home and trying to establish a new level of sexual connection based on truly loving another for his or her essence.

Touching souls is what we seek in all intimate relationships, sexual or otherwise. Through empathy we move from superficial connections to deep, heartfelt relationships that accept the whole person, imperfections and all. Ironically, when we are able to express this uncritical affection to others, we learn to accept ourselves with all our limitations and shortcomings in the process. We give to others and at the same time we are giving to ourselves. This is the path to unleashing the hold of *the curse*.

Keep Learning

I hope this book is a meaningful beginning on the road to changing your story and realizing your dreams. What matters is what works for you. Unlike a "program for quick recovery," it is important for you to travel at a pace that is workable and healthy for you.

It is through our relationships with others that we develop the skills to interact more empathically and build a more resilient sense of self. Always remember that any encounter can contribute to your learning—a person on the plane seat next to you, a new neighbor, a new friend or new associate. **Genuine relating breeds genuine change and growth.**

Many of my clients have been able to uncover driving aspects of their story, overcome addictions to performance, handle lifelong emotional trials and change errant thinking due to the open and honest feedback they have received. Therefore, one of my deepest motivations in writing this book was to tell the stories of my courageous clients.

I wanted to reach out and inspire more achievers who long for greater balance in their lives to take the risk and open their hearts to other people. Experiment with the concepts you have learned and it is quite likely you will become a "richer" and more satisfied person.

What Support is Right for You?

As we discussed, empathy is the capacity to understand and respond to the unique experiences of another. Without knowing you and your specific needs, I obviously cannot determine what the best course of action will be for you but the purpose of this book was to help you determine where your work is and to help you develop a game plan to begin the growth process. For individualized help, you can follow my work and access private coaching with me at http://www.balanceyoursuccess.com.

I invite you to visit us at http://www.thecurseofthecapable.com to contribute to our blog for support. I trust you will benefit from the ongoing insight and experiences shared by others who are changing their stories to experience the greatest emotional, physical, and spiritual well-being possible in their lives.

You will have the opportunity to ask questions, discover resources, read updated information and emerging insights regarding living a life free of "the curse".

Much success awaits you as you live the balanced, healthy, high-achieving life that is within your potential. I sincerely look forward to hearing from you in the near future.

An invitation to Change your Story and Balance Your Success

Now that you've read the book, we invite you to continue your journey with us and to utilize the added support available on our site.

Go to: www.TheCurseoftheCapable.com/ChangeYourStory to receive these valuable resources *and more*.

- Your FREE 30 day journal with inspiring quotes from Dr Ciaramicoli.

- Ongoing Teleseminars and Webinars that will help you change your story.

- Other valuable resources including weekly interactive blogs.

For private coaching with Dr. C, that will guide you in resolving those aspects of your original story that are preventing you from experiencing the love, health and balanced success you want, go to www.BalanceYourSuccess.com.

To learn *the lifestyle* mindset and skill set all balanced, healthy, high achieving people know and live by, with year-round support, go to www.PerformanceLifestyle.com.

Arthur P. Ciaramicoli, Ed.D., Ph.D.

 Arthur P. Ciaramicoli, Ed.D., Ph.D., is a licensed clinical psychologist who has been treating clients for more than 30 years. He is a member of the American Psychological Association and the Massachusetts Psychological Association. Currently in private practice, Dr. Ciaramicoli has been on the faculty of Harvard Medical School for several years, lecturer for the American Cancer Society, Chief Psychologist at Metrowest Medical Center, and director of the Metrowest Counseling Center and of the Alternative Medicine division of Metrowest Wellness Center in Framingham, Massachusetts.

In addition to treating patients, Dr. Ciaramicoli has lectured at Harvard Health Services, Boston College Counseling Center, the Space Telescope Science Institute in Baltimore as well as being a consultant to several major corporations in the Boston area.

Dr. Ciaramicoli is also a seasoned media expert. He has appeared on CNN, CNNfn, Fox News Boston, Comcast TV, New England Cable News, Good Morning America Weekend, The O'Reilly Report, and other shows. He has been a weekly radio guest on Your Healthy Family on Sirius Satellite Radio and Holistic Health Today, and has been interviewed on The People's Pharmacy, The Gary Null Show, and more than two dozen other radio programs airing on NPR, XM Radio, and numerous AM and FM stations.

Dr. Ciaramicoli is the author of *Performance Addiction: The Dangerous New Syndrome and How to Stop It from Ruining Your Life* (Wiley 2004) and *The Power of Empathy: A Practical Guide to Creating Intimacy, Self-Understanding, and Lasting Love* (Dutton 2000), which is now published in 7 languages and is soon to be released in Turkey.

His first book, *Treatment of Abuse and Addiction, A Holistic Approach* (Jason Aronson, 1997) was selected as Book of the Month by The Psychotherapy Book News.

He is also the coauthor of *Beyond the Influence: Understanding and Defeating Alcoholism* (Bantam 2000). Dr. Ciaramicoli lives in a suburb of Boston with his wife and two daughters.

John Allen Mollenhauer

John Allen Mollenhauer is one of the leading authorities in PerformanceLifestyle®, the antithesis of the performance addicted life.

As a trainer and coach, he is the founder of PerformanceLifestyle.com and the Lifestyle Coaching Center in Livingston, NJ. John Allen is a Professional Certified Coach, Certified Trainer with the International Sports Sciences Association, and Certified Nutritional Excellence Trainer.

As an entrepreneur he is also the founder of leading nutrition and fitness sites, NutrientRich.com and the social media site, MyTrainer.com.

RECOMMENDED READING

Albom, Mitch. Tuesdays with Morrie; An Old Man, a Young Man, and Life's Greatest Lesson. New York: Doubleday, 1997.

Ciaramicoli, Arthur, and Katherine Ketcham. The Power of Empathy: A Practical Guide to Creating Intimacy, Self-Understanding, and Lasting Love. New York: Plume, 2001

Ciaramicoli, Arthur. Performance Addiction: The Dangerous New Syndrome and How to Stop It from Ruining Your Life. New Jersey: Wiley, 2004

Begley, Sharon. Train Your Mind, Change Your Brain. New York: Ballantine, 2007.

Buettner, Dan. The Blue Zones: Lessons for Living Longer, From the People Who've Lived the Longest. Washington, D.C.: National Geographic Society, 2008

Bradshaw, John. Health the Shame That Binds You, Deerfield Beach FL, Health Communications, Inc., 1988

Emmons, Robert. Thanks: How Practicing Gratitude Can Make You Happy. New York: Houghton Mifflin, 2007.

Forni, P.M. The Civility Solution: What to Do When People Are Rude. New York: St. Martin's Press, 2008.

Gilbert, Daniel. Stumbling on Happiness. New York: Vintage Books, 2007.

Stefan, Klein. The Science of Happiness. New York: Marlowe and Company, 2002.

Pausch, Randy. The Last Lecture. New York: Hyperion, 2008

Pelletier, Kenneth. Sound Mind, Sound Body: A New Model for Lifelong Health. New York: Fireside, 1994.

Ratey, John. Spark: The Revolutionary New Science of Exercise and the Brain. New York: Little Brown, 2008.

Schreiber-Servan, David. Anti-Cancer: A New Way of Life. New York: Viking, 2008.

Smith, Huston. The Religions of Man, New York: Harper and Rowe, 1965.

Nhat Hanh, Thich. Living Buddha, Living Christ. New York: Riverhead, 1995.

Nhat Hanh, Thich. Going Home: Jesus and Buddha as Brothers. New York, Riverhead, 1999.